Learning CoreDNS
Configuring DNS for
Cloud Native Environments

John Belamaric and Cricket Liu

Beijing · Boston · Farnham · Sebastopol · Tokyo

Learning CoreDNS

by John Belamaric and Cricket Liu

Published by O'Reilly Media, Inc., 1005 Gravenstein Highway North, Sebastopol, CA 95472.

O'Reilly books may be purchased for educational, business, or sales promotional use. Online editions are also available for most titles (*http://oreilly.com*). For more information, contact our corporate/institutional sales department: 800-998-9938 or *corporate@oreilly.com*.

Acquisitions Editor: John Devins
Development Editor: Melissa Potter
Production Editor: Christopher Faucher
Copyeditor: Octal Publishing, LLC
Proofreader: Christina Edwards

Indexer: Ellen Troutman-Zaig
Interior Designer: David Futato
Cover Designer: Karen Montgomery
Illustrator: Rebecca Demarest

September 2019:   First Edition

Revision History for the First Edition

2019-08-30:   First Release

See *http://oreilly.com/catalog/errata.csp?isbn=9781492047964* for release details.

978-1-492-04796-4

[LSI]

Table of Contents

Preface

Why a New DNS Server?

Upon seeing this book, the first question that might occur to you is, "Why does the world need another DNS server?" There are, after all, lots of implementations of DNS servers to choose from. For starters, there's BIND, for Berkeley Internet Name Domain, the granddaddy of DNS servers. BIND has been around in some incarnation since the 1980s and supports just about every DNS standard written. There's Microsoft's DNS Server,[1] which is widely used in Active Directory environments. NSD from NLnet Labs and Knot are excellent authoritative DNS servers, and Unbound, also from NLnet Labs, is a fast, lean recursive DNS server. So what does CoreDNS offer that these others don't?

To begin with, CoreDNS is written in Go, and Go is a memory-safe programming language. Why is that important? Well, if you've ever run a BIND-based DNS infrastructure and had to upgrade 100 DNS servers ASAP because of a buffer overrun, you know. A healthy proportion of vulnerabilities in DNS servers of all stripes (at least those written in C and C++) stem from buffer overflows or overruns and dangling pointers. Written in memory-safe Go, CoreDNS isn't subject to these.

Programs written in Go can also support concurrency, or parallel execution. This can be useful in wringing more performance out of multiprocessing or multitasking systems. BIND's performance somewhat notoriously doesn't scale well on multiprocessor systems, whereas CoreDNS's performance scales nicely the more processors it has to work with.

---

1 Which wins the award for most prosaic name, hands-down.

Improving performance can be important because Go tends to run somewhat more slowly than C or C++,[2] partly thanks to the overhead imposed by its many features. In most cases, however, this isn't an issue: What's important is that CoreDNS performs well enough to handle the workload you offer it, and in the vast majority of cases, it does, Go or no Go.

Probably the most significant capability CoreDNS offers, though, is its ability to communicate with container infrastructure and orchestration systems such as etcd and Kubernetes.

Who Needs CoreDNS?

The short answer: basically anyone running Kubernetes, and most folks running containerized applications.

The function CoreDNS fulfills in a containerized environment is that of a service directory, which we talk about in detail in this book. A service directory helps containers determine the IP address or IP addresses where the containers that offer a particular service are running. For example, a container might look up a domain name that represents the database service for a specified application in order to retrieve some data. The service directory function is critical because, in the world of containers and microservices, applications are usually decomposed into many small services (hence, "microservices"!), and each service might be offered by several containers, each running at a different IP address.

But CoreDNS's utility isn't limited to containerized environments. CoreDNS's plugins support advanced DNS functionality that even the big boys like BIND don't support. You can rewrite queries and responses on the fly, for example. You can automatically load zone data from GitHub or Amazon Route 53. And because CoreDNS itself is small and usually runs in a container, it's suitable for use in scenarios in which a big DNS server such as BIND would not be.

---

2 Meaning that the same algorithm implemented the same way in Go, C, and C++ will probably run slightly faster in C and C++.

Who This Book Is For

This book is aimed at the following audiences:

- Administrators of containerized environments that need DNS-based service discovery, particularly when those environments are managed by Kubernetes.
- DNS administrators looking for a small, flexible DNS server that can run in a container.
- DNS administrators looking for a DNS server that
  — Integrates with Route 53
  — Supports flexible rewriting of queries and responses
  — Supports DNS over Transport Layer Security (TLS) and general-purpose Remote Procedure Call (gRPC)
- Developers looking to implement custom DNS functionality by writing their own CoreDNS plug-ins.

What You Will Learn

Readers of this book will learn:

- What distinguishes CoreDNS from other DNS servers
- Basic DNS theory, including the DNS namespace, domain names, zones, resource records, recursion, caching, and forwarding
- Basic CoreDNS configuration, including configuring common DNS servers such as primaries and secondaries and caching DNS servers
- CoreDNS's options for managing zone data, including advanced options such as loading from Git and Route 53
- How DNS-based service discovery works, and how to configure CoreDNS service discovery with etcd and Kubernetes
- How to rewrite queries and responses
- How to monitor and troubleshoot CoreDNS
- How to build custom versions of CoreDNS and write new plug-ins

Conventions Used in This Book

The following typographical conventions are used in this book:

Italic
: Indicates new terms, URLs, email addresses, filenames, and file extensions.

`Constant width`
: Used for program listings, as well as within paragraphs to refer to program elements such as variable or function names, databases, data types, environment variables, statements, and keywords.

> This element signifies a general note.

> This element indicates a warning or caution.

Using Code Examples

This book is here to help you get your job done. In general, if example code is offered with this book, you may use it in your programs and documentation. You do not need to contact us for permission unless you're reproducing a significant portion of the code. For example, writing a program that uses several chunks of code from this book does not require permission. Selling or distributing a CD-ROM of examples from O'Reilly books does require permission. Answering a question by citing this book and quoting example code does not require permission. Incorporating a significant amount of example code from this book into your product's documentation does require permission.

We appreciate, but do not require, attribution. An attribution usually includes the title, author, publisher, and ISBN. For example: "*Learning CoreDNS* by John Belamaric and Cricket Liu (O'Reilly). Copyright 2019 John Belamaric and Cricket Liu, 978-1-492-04796-4."

If you feel your use of code examples falls outside fair use or the permission given above, feel free to contact us at *permissions@oreilly.com*.

O'Reilly Online Learning

 For almost 40 years, *O'Reilly Media* has provided technology and business training, knowledge, and insight to help companies succeed.

Our unique network of experts and innovators share their knowledge and expertise through books, articles, conferences, and our online learning platform. O'Reilly's online learning platform gives you on-demand access to live training courses, in-depth learning paths, interactive coding environments, and a vast collection of text and video from O'Reilly and 200+ other publishers. For more information, please visit *http://oreilly.com*.

How to Contact Us

Please address comments and questions concerning this book to the publisher:

O'Reilly Media, Inc.
1005 Gravenstein Highway North
Sebastopol, CA 95472
800-998-9938 (in the United States or Canada)
707-829-0515 (international or local)
707-829-0104 (fax)

We have a web page for this book, where we list errata, examples, and any additional information: *https://oreil.ly/learning-coreDNS*.

To comment or ask technical questions about this book, please send an email to *bookquestions@oreilly.com*.

For more information about our books, courses, conferences, and news, see our website at *http://www.oreilly.com*.

Find us on Facebook: *http://facebook.com/oreilly*

Follow us on Twitter: *http://twitter.com/oreillymedia*

Watch us on YouTube: *http://www.youtube.com/oreillymedia*

Acknowledgments

The authors would like to thank their able reviewers Miek Gieben, François Tur, and Michael Grosser for catching errors both subtle and egregious. They would also like to thank all the other members of the CoreDNS community for creating such an incredible product.

John would like to thank his amazing wife, Robin, for her support, encouragement, and assistance. He couldn't have done it without her. He also would like to acknowledge the support of his son, Owen, and daughter, Audrey, who have put up with all the nonsense that goes along with their dad writing a book. He gives thanks to Tim Hockin, Bowei Du, and the rest of the Kubernetes SIG-Network team for helping guide CoreDNS into Kubernetes, and to his former colleagues at Infoblox, particularly Chris O'Haver and Sandeep Rajan, who worked hard to make CoreDNS the right choice for Kubernetes. Finally, he would like to thank his former colleague Alan Conley, without whose support, CoreDNS would not be what it is today.

Cricket would like to acknowledge his friends and colleagues at Infoblox, particularly his boss, Alan Conley. Without Alan's regular harassment, this book would never have gotten off the ground. And he sends his love and thanks to Kristin, for her steadfast support; to his kids, Walt (née Walter B) and Greta (née Baby G), sources of amusement and amazement and no small amount of eye-rolling; and, finally, to Charlie and Jessie, who provided sisterly canine companionship through much of this project but, sadly, didn't make it to see the end.

## CHAPTER 1

Introduction

This book is about CoreDNS, a new DNS server that's been designed to work well with containers, such as Linux and Docker containers, and especially well in environments managed by Kubernetes, the popular container orchestration system.

This first chapter explains CoreDNS's *raison d'être*, and how it differs from other DNS servers, including its limitations. The chapter also covers a little of the history of CoreDNS, such as its relationship to the Cloud Native Computing Foundation.

What Is CoreDNS?

CoreDNS is DNS server software that's often used to support the service discovery function in containerized environments, particularly those managed by Kubernetes. Miek Gieben wrote the original version of CoreDNS in 2016. He'd previously written a DNS server called SkyDNS and a popular library of DNS functions in the Go language called Go DNS. Like its successor, CoreDNS, SkyDNS's main purpose was to support service discovery. But Miek admired the architecture of a Go-based web server called Caddy, so he forked Caddy to create CoreDNS. CoreDNS thus inherited the major advantages of Caddy: its simple configuration syntax, its powerful plug-in-based architecture, and its foundation in Go.

Compared to the syntax of, say, BIND's configuration file, CoreDNS's *Corefile*, as it's called, is refreshingly simple. The Corefile for a basic CoreDNS-based DNS server is often just a few lines long and—relatively speaking—easy to read.

CoreDNS uses plug-ins to provide DNS functionality. So there's a plug-in for caching and a plug-in for forwarding, a plug-in for configuring a primary DNS server that reads zone data from a file and a plug-in for configuring a secondary DNS server. Not only is configuring each plug-in straightforward (see the previous paragraph), but if you don't need a plug-in, you don't configure it and its code isn't executed. That makes CoreDNS faster and more secure.

Plug-ins are also fairly easy to develop. That's important for two reasons. First, if you want to extend CoreDNS's functionality, you can write your own plug-in; we cover that in Chapter 9. Second, because writing new plug-ins isn't rocket science, many have been developed, and more are being written all the time. You might find one that provides functionality you need.

The Go language is "memory-safe," which means that it's protected from "memory access errors" such as buffer overflows and dangling pointers. That's particularly important for a DNS server such as CoreDNS, which anyone on the internet could conceivably access. A malicious actor might exploit a buffer overflow to crash a DNS server or even to gain control of the underlying operating system (OS). In fact, over the decades of its history, a substantial number of the serious vulnerabilities in BIND have been caused by memory access errors. With CoreDNS, you don't need to worry about those.

Probably the most significant advantage CoreDNS offers, though, is its ability to communicate with container infrastructure and orchestration systems such as etcd and Kubernetes. We discuss this in much more detail later in the book, but let's take a quick look at this functionality here.

CoreDNS, Containers, and Microservices

If you're in the tiny subset of humanity to whom this book appeals, you've probably heard of containers. If you haven't, think of a container as a very lightweight, efficient virtual machine (VM). Whereas VMs can share a single hardware platform, courtesy of a *hypervisor*, containers provide execution environments that run under the same OS kernel but provide a similar level of isolation as VMs. Containers are much smaller than VMs and can be started and stopped much more quickly.

Containers are often used in software based on a *microservices* architecture. With microservices, an application, often a complex one, is decomposed into many micro-services. Each microservice is responsible for providing a small but useful and clearly defined set of functionality. For example, one microservice might handle authentica-tion of users, whereas another manages authorization of those users. An application, in total, might comprise dozens or hundreds of microservices, communicating with one another over a network.

In practice, each microservice might be provided by one or more containers. The authentication service, for example, might be implemented as a container. It's so quick and easy to start and stop containers that the application—or a higher-level *con-tainer orchestrator*—might start and stop additional authentication containers dynam-ically as demand for authentication waxes and wanes.

In such an environment, though, tracking where a particular service is running can be challenging. Say a container supporting the database service needs to communicate with the authorization service to determine whether a given user should be allowed to conduct a particular search. If the containers that implement the authorization service are being started and stopped dynamically to accommodate load, how do we get a list of all running authorization containers?

The answer is most often DNS, the Domain Name System. Since the communications between containers is almost always based on IP, the Internet Protocol, and because developers have been using DNS to find the IP addresses of resources for literally decades, using DNS to identify containers that offer a given service is natural.

It's in this capacity that CoreDNS really shines. Not only is CoreDNS a flexible, secure DNS server, but it integrates directly with many container orchestration systems, including Kubernetes. This means that it's easy for the administrators of containerized applications to set up a DNS server to mediate and facilitate communications between containers.

CoreDNS Limitations

CoreDNS does currently have some significant limitations, though, and it won't be suitable for every conceivable DNS server. Chief among these is that CoreDNS, at least in the latest version as of this writing, doesn't support full *recursion*. In other words, CoreDNS can't process a query by starting at the root of a DNS namespace, querying a root DNS server and following referrals until it gets an answer from one of the authoritative DNS servers. Instead, it relies on other DNS servers—usually called *forwarders*—for that. In Chapter 2, we talk more about recursion and forwarders.

If you're still on the fence about whether CoreDNS is the right choice for your particular needs, Table 1-1 might help; it summarizes the key differences between CoreDNS's functionality and BIND's.

Table 1-1. Key functional differences between CoreDNS and BIND

	CoreDNS	BIND
Full recursion	No	Yes
Dynamic updates	No	Yes
Integration with Kubernetes	Yes	No
Integration with Amazon Route 53	Yes	No
Domain Name System Security Extensions (DNSSEC) support	Limited	Full
Support for DNS over Transport Layer Security (DoT)	Yes	No

If you're unsure about what some of these terms mean, don't worry, we cover them later in the book. Before we do, though, let's talk briefly about the formal relationship between CoreDNS, Kubernetes, and something called the Cloud Native Computing Foundation.

CoreDNS, Kubernetes, and the Cloud Native Computing Foundation

Kubernetes, the container orchestration system with which CoreDNS integrates so nicely, was originally written at Google and then converted to an open source project in 2015. To manage the newly open sourced Kubernetes, Google partnered with The Linux Foundation to create the Cloud Native Computing Foundation, or CNCF for short.

The CNCF has become the home for many technologies important to building cloud-based applications, including Prometheus, which supports collecting metrics and alerting, and Envoy, a service proxy. Projects managed by the CNCF move through various "maturity levels," from "sandbox," for early-stage projects; to "incubating," for projects gaining acceptance; to "graduated," for mature projects suitable for broad adoption.

CoreDNS was submitted to the CNCF in 2017 and moved to "graduated" status in January 2019. As testament to CoreDNS's criticality to Kubernetes environments, CoreDNS became the default DNS server shipped with Kubernetes with Kubernetes version 1.13, which was released in December 2018. Given that CoreDNS is now installed with almost every new Kubernetes implementation, and Kubernetes is a juggernaut in the world of containers (and containers themselves seem to be taking the world by storm), we expect the installed base of CoreDNS to explode.

Enough of singing CoreDNS's praises. We've talked about what CoreDNS is good for and what it isn't, and how it's had its fate lashed to Kubernetes. Next, we give you a whirlwind refresher on DNS theory so that we can begin talking about how to configure CoreDNS to do useful work!

## CHAPTER 2

A DNS Refresher

So far, we've talked about practical matters like what CoreDNS is, what's it's good at (vis-à-vis DNS functionality) and what it's not good at. Of course, that discussion had to include some DNS terminology—terminology that, in fairness, not everyone is familiar with.

We deliberated for a while over how much DNS theory to include in this book. We could, of course, "Begin at the beginning, and go on till... the end, then stop," but that's been done in other books, including books we've written. Still, it didn't seem fair to send you out into the world without at least a grounding in DNS.

Our compromise is to try to give you *just enough* DNS theory to get by, and then to point you in the direction of, for example, *DNS and BIND* if you're interested in more detail. (Hopefully that doesn't seem too self-serving.)

What Is the Domain Name System?

The DNS is a naming system that maps names to other data, such as IP addresses, mail routing information, and more. And DNS isn't just any naming system: it's the internet's standard naming system as well as one of the largest distributed databases in the world.

DNS is also a client–server system, with DNS clients querying DNS servers to retrieve data stored in that distributed database. Because the database is distributed, DNS servers will often need to query one or more other DNS servers to find a given piece of data. DNS clients are often called *resolvers*, whereas DNS servers are sometimes called *name servers*.[1] Resolvers ask DNS servers for information about particular indexes into the distributed database.

Domain Names and the Namespace

Those indexes into DNS's distributed database are called *domain names*. These are the dotted names that should be familiar to you from internet email addresses and URLs. In an email address, the domain name appears to the right of the "@" sign. In a URL, the domain name appears after the "://" and before the next "/," if any. So in the email address cricket@foo.example, "foo.example" is the domain name. In the URL http://www.bar.example/, "www.bar.example" is the domain name.

These domain names actually represent nodes in DNS's *namespace*. DNS's namespace is an inverted tree, with the root node at the top. Each node can have an arbitrarily large number of child nodes, and is usually depicted with links between it and its children. Each node also has a label, which can be up to 63 ASCII characters long. The root node has a special label: the null label, which has zero length. Only the root node has the null label. Beyond that, there aren't many restrictions on labels—mainly that the child nodes of a single node must all have different labels. That makes sense: It helps avoid ambiguity and confusion, just as giving your children unique first names does.[2] Figure 2-1 shows a portion of a fictional DNS namespace to help illustrate these concepts.

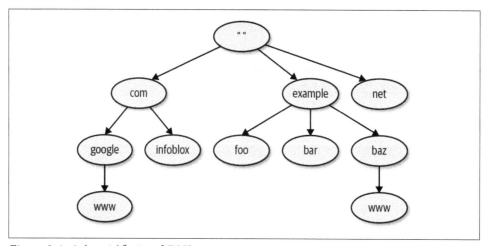

Figure 2-1. A (semi-)fictional DNS namespace

---

1 We'll refer to them as DNS servers in this book, though in other books we referred to them as name servers. People change!

2 And yes, George Foreman is the canonical counterexample of this. But George's five sons named "George" all have name suffixes (II, III, etc.) and nicknames to help tell them apart.

Clearly a label is useful only in distinguishing one node from its siblings; some other identifier is needed to identify a particular node in the entire namespace. That identifier is the domain name.

A node's domain name is the list of labels on the path from that node upward to the root of the namespace, with a single dot separating each label from the next. For example, in Figure 2-2, the indicated node has the domain name www.baz.example.

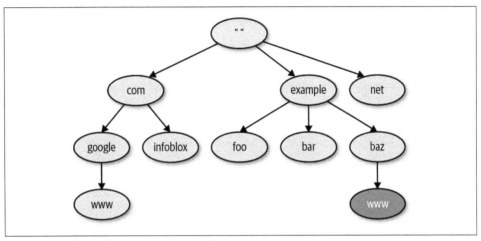

Figure 2-2. The node www.baz.example

Once upon a time, in the early days of the internet, domain names at the bottom of the namespace (the "leaves" of the tree, if you will) represented individual hosts. Nowadays, that's less and less true. Individual hosts do have domain names, of course (though in some cases they can have more than just one), but domain names can represent the following:

- Websites, such as *www.google.com*, which can be served by many individual hosts
- Email destinations, such as *gmail.com*, which again can be served by many hosts
- Other resources not necessarily tied to a single host, such as an FTP service
- Some combination of these. *infoblox.com*, for example, is a website, an email destination, and more

Next, let's look at how domain names are grouped, and how they're managed.

Domains, Delegation, and Zones

There are a few other bits of theory we need to introduce before diving into the world of how DNS servers work, so please bear with us. The first is a *domain*. A domain is a group of nodes in a particular subtree of the namespace; that is, at or below a particular node. The domain is identified by the node at its apex (the topmost node in the domain): it has the same domain name. For example, Figure 2-3 shows the domain *foo.example*, with the node *foo.example* at its apex.

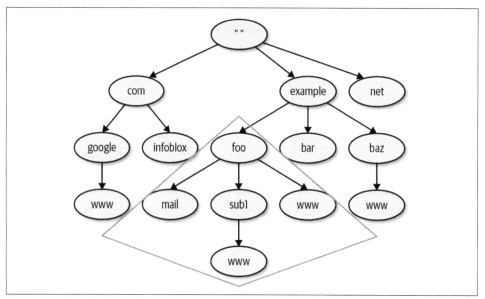

Figure 2-3. The domain foo.example

Given that *foo.example* can indicate either the node and the domain, it's important that we specify the context when identifying it: the node *foo.example* or the domain *foo.example*.

In practice, domains are usually managed by particular organizations. For example, Google manages *google.com*, Infoblox manages *infoblox.com*, and UC Berkeley manages *berkeley.edu*. This means that these organizations can create new nodes in their domain and attach data to those nodes. (More on that to come.)

Sometimes, an organization wants to allow a different organization to manage a portion of their domain. For example, the folks at UC Berkeley who run *berkeley.edu* might decide that their computer science (CS) department is capable of running a portion of *berkeley.edu* themselves, and that allowing the CS department to do so directly would avoid the unnecessary headache of having the CS department request changes to *berkeley.edu* through some central authority.[3]

This is accomplished through *delegation*. The folks in Berkeley's IT department can create a subdomain of *berkeley.edu*, which is simply a subtree of the *berkeley.edu*

---

3 Berkeley historically has not been fond of central authority.

domain, and delegate it to the CS department. They might well name it something intuitive, such as *cs.berkeley.edu* (and in fact they have).

We'll leave aside for the time being the mechanics of how delegation is done. For now, suffice it to say that the *berkeley.edu* domain now contains information on where people can find information in the *cs.berkeley.edu* subdomain, rather than containing that information itself.

Thanks to delegation, the IT folks at Berkeley no longer control nodes at or below *cs.berkeley.edu*; those belong to the CS department. What do we call the set of nodes at or below *berkeley.edu* that the IT folks still control? That's the *berkeley.edu zone*. A zone is a domain minus the subdomains that have been delegated elsewhere. What if there's no delegation within a domain? In that case, the domain and the zone contain the same nodes. For example, if there's no further delegation below *cs.berkeley.edu*, the domain *cs.berkeley.edu* and the zone *cs.berkeley.edu* are effectively the same.

There are zones *above berkeley.edu*, too, of course. The *edu* domain is run by a nonprofit association called EDUCAUSE, which delegates *berkeley.edu* and *umich.edu* and many other subdomains to educational institutions around the world. What they're left with—what they directly manage—is the *edu* zone.

Okay, we've covered the structure of the indexes into DNS's distributed database. But what about the data?

Resource Records

If, as we said, DNS is a distributed database, where's all the data? So far, we have indexes (domain names) and partitions of the database (zones), but no actual data.

Data in DNS is stored in units of *resource records*. Resource records come in different classes and types. The classes were intended to allow DNS to function as the naming service for different kinds of networks, but in practice DNS is used only on the internet and TCP/IP networks, so just one class, "IN," for internet, is used.[4] The types of resource records in the IN class specify both the format and application of the data stored. Here's a list of some of the most common resource record types in the IN class:

A (IPv4 address)
   Maps a domain name to a single IPv4 address

AAAA (IPv6 address)
   Maps a domain name to a single IPv6 address

---

4 For those of you jumping up and down, shouting about Hesiod and Chaosnet, sit down, both of you.

CNAME (alias)
    Maps a domain name (the alias) to another domain name (the canonical name)

MX (mail exchanger)
    Names a mail exchanger (mail server) for an email destination

NS (name server)
    Names a name server (or DNS server) for a zone

PTR (pointer)
    Maps an IP address back to a domain name

SOA (start of authority)
    Provides parameters for a zone

Each record type requires record-specific data, called RDATA for short, in a particular format. For example, an A record requires RDATA of a single, 32-bit IPv4 address. When you see A records in zone data files (more on them later) or in the output of various tools, the RDATA will usually be formatted as a dotted-octet value (e.g., 192.168.0.1). Similarly, a AAAA (pronounced "quad A") record takes a single, 128-bit address as RDATA, which in zone data files is usually formatted in the standard, colon-separated hexadecimal format used for IPv6 addresses (e.g., 2001:db8:ac10:fe01::1).

There are dozens of types besides the seven in this list, and many with more complex RDATA formats than A and AAAA. We cover the format and semantics of resource records at the end of this chapter For now, let's move on to the types of DNS servers.

DNS Servers and Authority

DNS servers have two chief responsibilities: answering queries about domain names, and querying other DNS servers about domain names. Let's begin with the first responsibility: answering queries.

DNS servers can load zone data from files called, appropriately enough, *zone data files* or, equivalently, *master files*. Each zone data file contains a complete description of a zone: all of the records attached to all of the domain names in the zone. A DNS server that loads information about a zone from a zone data file is called a *primary DNS server* for that zone.

DNS servers can also load zone data from other DNS servers via a mechanism called a *zone transfer*. A DNS server that loads information about a zone from another DNS server using zone transfer is said to be a secondary DNS server for that zone. The DNS server from which the secondary DNS server transfers the zone is referred to as its *master DNS server*. After transferring the zone, the secondary DNS server might save a copy of the zone data to disk, sometimes in what's called a *backup zone data file.* When the secondary periodically transfers a new version of the zone from its master DNS server, it updates the data on disk. The backup data is useful if the secondary DNS server should restart because it can initially load the backup data, then check to see whether that data is still up to date with the version of the zone on the master DNS server. If it is, no zone transfer is necessary. And if the master DNS server is unavailable, the secondary DNS server still has zone data it can answer with.

Figure 2-4 shows you the relationship between primary and secondary DNS servers.

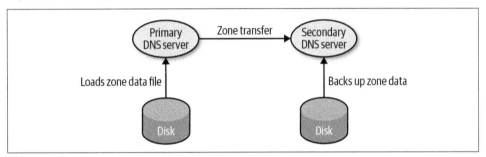

Figure 2-4. The relationship between primary and secondary DNS servers

Both the primary and secondary DNS servers for a zone are said to be *authoritative* for the zone. This means that they can answer any query for a domain name in the zone definitively. (Other DNS servers, you'll see, might have cached answers to queries, which might or might not still be current.)

A single DNS server can be authoritative for many zones at the same time and can be primary for some and secondary for others. Internet service providers and DNS hosting companies often run DNS servers that are authoritative for hundreds of thousands of zones.

That's enough about DNS servers for now. Let's move on to resolvers, the other main software component of the Domain Name System.

Resolvers

Resolvers are the client half of the DNS. Unlike DNS servers, they're often not distinct pieces of software. Instead, they're functionality built in to an OS such as Windows, MacOS X, or iOS.[5] Even very simple internet devices usually have resolvers built in to their firmware.

Resolvers take applications' requests for information about a domain name and translate them into DNS queries. They then send those queries to DNS servers and

---

5 In Unix-y operating systems, the resolver is often part of the standard shared C library, libc, or glibc.

await responses. If the resolver doesn't receive a response to a given query within a reasonable amount of time (typically a second or a few seconds at most), it might retransmit the query to the same DNS server, or it might try querying a different DNS server. When it receives a response, the resolver unpacks it into a data structure that it passes back to the application. Some resolvers do even more, including caching recently returned answers.

Resolvers are useful because they obviate the need for all applications that need DNS data to speak the DNS protocol, which isn't particularly friendly. Instead, applications can use well-defined library functions such as `getaddrinfo()` or `gethostbyname()` to request the information they need about a domain name, and can then retrieve that information in a straightforward way. Resolvers aren't very useful *by themselves*, though: they need DNS servers to help them perform their function.

Resolution and Recursion

Resolution is the process by which resolvers and DNS servers cooperate to find answers (in the form of resource records) stored in DNS's distributed database. Sometimes resolution is simple: A resolver sends a query to a DNS server on behalf of an application, and the DNS server is authoritative for the zone that contains the domain name in the query, so it responds directly to the resolver with the records that make up the answer. However, for cases in which the DNS server isn't authoritative for the zone that contains the answer, the resolution process is more complicated.

By default, the resolution process proceeds from the top of the DNS namespace down. Remember that the namespace is an inverted tree: Starting at the top of the inverted tree, you can reach any node. And the domain name in the query tells the DNS server which "branch" to take from each node, as shown in Figure 2-5.

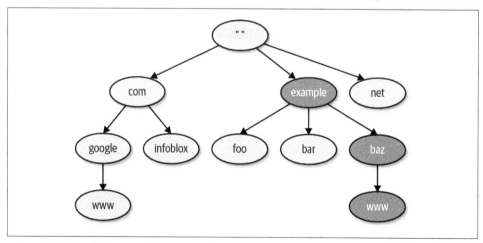

Figure 2-5. Resolving www.baz.example

DNS servers need a "hint" to direct them where to start, though. Clearly, they should start at the root, but which DNS servers are authoritative for the root zone? That information is provided by the *root hints*, which are usually either compiled into a DNS server or contained in a file. The hints themselves are NS records, which we mentioned earlier: these records give the domain names of the DNS servers authoritative for the root zone. Each of the NS records has a corresponding A and AAAA record, providing the IPv4 and IPv6 address of each root DNS server. Example 2-1 shows what the beginning of the current root hints file looks like.

Example 2-1. Beginning of the current root hints file

```
;
; FORMERLY NS.INTERNIC.NET
;
.                       3600000     NS      A.ROOT-SERVERS.NET.
A.ROOT-SERVERS.NET.     3600000     A       198.41.0.4
A.ROOT-SERVERS.NET.     3600000     AAAA    2001:503:ba3e::2:30
;
; FORMERLY NS1.ISI.EDU
;
.                       3600000     NS      B.ROOT-SERVERS.NET.
B.ROOT-SERVERS.NET.     3600000     A       199.9.14.201
B.ROOT-SERVERS.NET.     3600000     AAAA    2001:500:200::b
```

This excerpt shows just two of the 13 root DNS servers, *a.root-servers.net* and *b.root-servers.net*, as well as their addresses. The single dots (".") at the beginning of the two NS records stand for the root zone, whereas the dots at the end of the domain names of the root DNS servers unambiguously anchor those domain names to the root of the namespace, a bit like a leading slash in a pathname (*/etc/hosts*) anchors that pathname to the root of the filesystem. The numerical fields (3600000) are the time-to-live values for the records, which we discuss shortly.

A DNS server can start resolution by sending a query to any of the root DNS servers. The root DNS server probably won't be authoritative for the zone containing the domain name in the query, but will at least know the DNS servers authoritative for the top-level zone (e.g., *com, net*) the domain name falls under. The root DNS server will return the list of DNS servers authoritative for the appropriate top-level zone in a *referral* to the querying DNS server. The referral contains yet more NS records, these for the top-level zone.

The DNS server continues by querying one of the DNS servers for the top-level zone, following referrals until it reaches the DNS servers authoritative for the domain name in the query. When it queries one of those DNS servers, it should receive an answer instead of a referral, as shown in Figure 2-6.

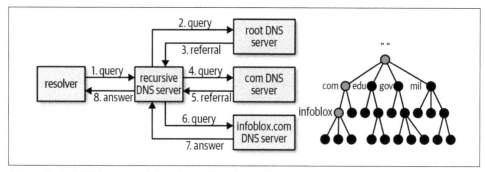

Figure 2-6. A DNS server following referrals until receiving an answer

The process that the first DNS server follows—starting with the root DNS servers and following referrals until it receives an answer—is called *recursion*. Note that the other DNS servers in the process—the DNS servers that return the referrals—don't perform recursion. For example, the root DNS server doesn't query a DNS server authoritative for the top-level zone on behalf of the first DNS server. The root DNS server simply replies with the most useful information it already has, NS records from its authoritative zone data. That's because resolvers generally send recursive queries to DNS servers, whereas DNS servers send nonrecursive, or iterative, queries to each other by default. Accepting a recursive query obliges a DNS server to do whatever work is necessary to answer the query, including possibly following several levels of referrals. A DNS server receiving a nonrecursive query need only respond with a referral to help the querying DNS server on its way.

There's one case in which a DNS server sends another DNS server a recursive query, and that's when the first DNS server is configured to use the second as a *forwarder*. When configured to use a forwarder, a DNS server that receives a query first looks in its authoritative zone data and cache for an answer, and if it doesn't find one, it forwards the query to its forwarder.[6]

Forwarders are often used to provide the ability to resolve domain names in the internet's namespace to DNS servers without direct connectivity to the internet: the "internal" DNS servers are configured to use a DNS server with internet connectivity as a forwarder.

Whoops, we slipped a little earlier. We said that DNS servers configured to use forwarders check their authoritative zone data and cache before consulting a forwarder. What is this "cache" of which we speak?

---

6 You might have noticed that the terminology is backward: The DNS server that forwards the query should, by rights, be called the forwarder. Instead, it's the DNS server that receives the forwarded query that's called the forwarder.

Caching

If all recursive DNS resolution had to start with the root DNS servers, resolution would take a long time. There are only 13 root DNS servers, after all, so in addition to lengthening the resolution process, starting at the roots would overwhelm them with queries.[7]

In practice, most DNS servers processing recursive queries don't need to query the root DNS servers very often. That's because they cache the resource records in responses.

As you saw in the root hints file, resource records have time-to-live values associated with them. That time-to-live value is an indication to recursive DNS servers of how long they can cache those records. Take a recursive DNS server that's worked its way down to the *google.com* DNS servers to resolve *www.google.com*'s AAAA records. Along the way, it's learned:

- The domain names and (IPv4 and IPv6) addresses of the DNS servers authoritative for *com*
- The domain names and addresses of the DNS servers authoritative for *google.com*
- The IPv6 addresses of *www.google.com*

Should the same DNS server receive a query for *maps.google.com* soon afterward, it can skip querying a root DNS server or a *com* DNS server and query a *google.com* DNS server first, reducing query load on the root and *com* DNS servers and shortening the resolution time substantially. Similarly, resolving *infoblox.com*'s MX records could begin at the *com* DNS servers, saving at least the roundtrip to a root DNS server.

Next, let's go back for a closer look at resource records, which store the data in the DNS namespace.

Resource Records

We introduced several types of resource records earlier in this chapter, and you've even seen a few in what's called their *master file format*: the NS, A and AAAA records in the root hints file. Master file format is the format in which resource records appear in zone data files: primary DNS servers read zone data in this format, as do secondary DNS servers (when they read backup zone data files).

---

7 This actually a lie. Each of the 13 root DNS servers is actually a distributed group of DNS servers that share a single IP address using a technique called anycast. But they could still be overwhelmed.

Records in master file format have the following general format:

```
[NAME] [TTL] [CLASS] TYPE RDATA
```

We walk through each field in the following sections, starting with the NAME field.

NAME

The NAME field contains the domain name to which this resource record is attached. This can be a *fully qualified domain name* (FQDN), ending in a dot, or a *relative domain name*, which doesn't end in a dot. Relative domain names are interpreted as ending in the current *origin*, which by default is the domain name of the zone that the zone data file describes. That's handy, because if you're writing the zone data file for *foo.example*, you'd rather not have to type "foo.example" at the end of each name.

If you want to refer to the origin itself, rather than have it appended to the name you type, you use "@" in the NAME field, with no trailing dot. You can also use a single dot (".") to refer to the root, though you usually wouldn't use that in the NAME field of a resource record unless you were editing the root zone data file or root hints file.

As you can see from the format we showed you a moment ago, the NAME field is optional. If the NAME field is omitted, the line must start with whitespace, and the resource record specified on the line is attached to the most recently specified domain name.

Example 2-2 demonstrates some NAME fields.

Example 2-2. NAME fields in the foo.example zone data file

```
@             3600  IN  A  10.0.0.1  # Attached to foo.example, the origin
foo.example.  3600  IN  A  10.0.0.2  # Also attached to foo.example
www           3600  IN  A  10.0.0.3  # Attached to www.foo.example
              3600  IN  A  10.0.0.4  # Also attached to www.foo.example
```

Next comes the TTL field.

TTL

The TTL field specifies the time-to-live (TTL) value for the resource record, which governs how long a recursive DNS server can cache the record. The TTL is natively (i.e., on the wire) a 32-bit integer number of seconds, and you can specify TTLs that way, but you can now also use scaling factors such as "s" for seconds, "m" for minutes, "h" for hours, "d" for days, and "w" for weeks, as in "1d," "30m," or "1h30m." This will obviate the need for you to waste precious brain capacity remembering things like "There are 86400 seconds in a day."

If the TTL is not specified for a resource record, the record inherits the most recently specified TTL value. Example 2-3 shows the TTL field in action.

Example 2-3. TTL fields in the foo.example zone data file

```
@          3600  IN  A  10.0.0.1  # TTL of 3600 seconds, or 1 hour
           1h    IN  A  10.0.0.2  # Same thing
www        1h30m IN  A  10.0.0.3  # TTL of 1 hour and 30 minutes, or 90 minutes
                 IN  A  10.0.0.4  # TTL from precious record, so 90 minutes
```

After the TTL field comes the CLASS field.

CLASS

As stated previously in this chapter, the CLASS field is almost always IN, for internet, so it should come as no surprise that IN is the default. There are other classes, such as CH for ChaosNet and HS for Hesiod, but you'll rarely see them in use, because the functions those other classes were meant to serve never took off.

Resource Record Types

The resource record types that we introduced earlier, such as A for an IPv4 address and AAAA for an IPv6 address, are properly called *type mnemonics*. Each resource record type has a unique type mnemonic. On the wire, the type mnemonic translates into a numeric type code, but it's much easier to remember the mnemonic (or they wouldn't call it a mnemonic, would they?).

As we said earlier, each resource record type requires a certain syntax for the data that follows the type mnemonic, called RDATA. Let's go through some of the most common record types and their RDATA syntax.

The A Record

The A record maps the domain name to which it's attached to a single IPv4 address. Consequently, the A record's RDATA field is a single IPv4 address in dotted-octet notation, as demonstrated in Example 2-4.

Example 2-4. An A record

```
www.foo.example.  300  IN  A  10.0.0.1
```

To map a single domain name to multiple IPv4 addresses, you simply add multiple A records to the domain name, as shown in Example 2-5.

Example 2-5. Multiple A records

```
www  1h  IN  A  10.0.0.1
     1h  IN  A  10.0.1.1
```

The AAAA Record

Like the A record, the AAAA record maps the domain name to which it's attached to an IP address, but an IPv6 address rather than an IPv4 address. The AAAA record's RDATA field, then, contains a single IPv6 address in the standard, colon-separated, hexadecimal notation,[8] as illustrated in Example 2-6.

Example 2-6. An AAAA record

```
www  30m  IN  AAAA  2001:db8:42:1:1
```

As with A records, to map a single domain name to multiple IPv6 addresses, you just add multiple AAAA records to the domain name, as shown in Example 2-7.

Example 2-7. Multiple AAAA records

```
www  30m  IN  AAAA  2001:db8:42:1:1
     30m  IN  AAAA  2001:db8:42:2:1
```

The CNAME Record

You use the CNAME record to create an alias from one domain name to another. The CNAME record is attached to the domain name that is the alias; the CNAME record's RDATA is the domain name that the alias points to, called a *canonical name* (hence, "CNAME"). Example 2-8 demonstrates how it works.

Example 2-8. A CNAME record

```
alias.foo.example.  1d  IN  CNAME  canonicalname.foo.example.
```

There are several rules that govern the use of CNAME records:

- The domain name that is the alias can't have any other record types attached to it. That's because of the way DNS servers process CNAME records: a recursive DNS server looking up *alias.foo.example*'s AAAA records, for example, would receive the record in Example 2-8 from an authoritative DNS server for *foo.example*. The recursive DNS server would then restart the query, this time looking for AAAA

---

8 This is described in RFC 4291, if you're interested.

records for *canonicalname.foo.example*. If attaching a AAAA record directly to *alias.foo.example* were permitted, the results of looking up AAAA records for *alias.foo.example* would be ambiguous.

- A corollary to the preceding rule is that the domain name of a zone (e.g., *foo.example*) can't own a CNAME record, because by definition it must own a start of authority (SOA) record.
- CNAME records can point one alias to another alias, but you should be careful not to create a loop (*a* is an alias for *b* and *b* is an alias for *a*), and you shouldn't create too long a chain of aliases, because recursive DNS servers typically limit the number of CNAME records that they'll follow.

The MX Record

You use the MX record to direct email addressed to a particular domain name; in particular, it designates *mail exchangers* (hence, "MX") for a domain name.

When a mail transport agent (or MTA) has an email message addressed to some *user@domain.name*, it must determine where to send that message. The MTA could just look up the A or AAAA records for *domain.name*, but MTAs on the internet look up MX records first. (They often fall back to looking up A and AAAA records if no MX records are available.)

An MX record specifies the domain name of a mail exchanger for a domain name and a preference value associated with that mail exchanger. The preference is an unsigned, 16-bit value, so between 0 and 65535, in decimal terms. (The preference actually precedes the mail exchanger.) Example 2-9 shows an MX record.

Example 2-9. An MX record

```
foo.example.  3d  IN  MX  10 mail.isp.net.
```

This MX record tells an MTA, "If you have an email message addressed to a user at *foo.example* such as *cricket@foo.example*), send it to *mail.isp.net*. It's handy to be able to specify the domain name of a mail exchanger rather than its address because nowadays so many organizations use email hosting services rather than running their own mail servers, and you wouldn't want to have to track changes your hosting service made to the addresses of its mail servers.

The preference value is significant only if a domain name owns multiple MX records. In that case, an MTA is supposed to sort the MX records it finds for the domain name, lowest preference value (i.e., closest to zero) to highest preference value, and attempt delivery first to the mail exchanger with the lowest value. The MTA can try a mail exchanger at a higher preference value only after it has attempted delivery to all mail exchangers with lower preference values. This makes it possible to list backup mail servers for your domain name, as shown in Example 2-10.

Example 2-10. Multiple MX records

```
@   3d   IN   MX   0 mail.foo.example.
    3d   IN   MX   10 mail.isp.net.
```

The NS Record

The NS record is somewhat similar to an MX record: it designates a *name server* for a given zone. The NS record's RDATA is the domain name of a DNS server authoritative for the zone to which the record is attached. For example, the NS record in Example 2-11 says that you'll find a DNS server authoritative for *foo.example* running at *ns1.foo.example*:

Example 2-11. NS record

```
foo.example.  1d   IN   NS   ns1.foo.example.
```

Unlike most types of resource records, NS records attached to a given domain name typically appear in two different zones: the zone with the specified domain name and in that zone's parent zone. Take the *foo.example* NS record in Example 2-11. We'd find it in the *foo.example* zone, of course, but also in the *example* zone.

In the *example* zone, the NS record is responsible for delegating the *foo.example* sub-zone to *ns1.foo.example*. In fact, it's probably part of a larger set of NS records for *foo.example*, as shown in Example 2-12.

Example 2-12. Multiple NS records

```
foo.example.  1d   IN   NS   ns1.foo.example.
              1d   IN   NS   ns2.foo.example.
              1d   IN   NS   ns1.isp.net.
```

A DNS server authoritative for the *example* zone would return these NS records any time it was queried for a domain name in *foo.example*, effectively saying, "If you're interested in domain names that end in *foo.example*, you should talk to one of these three DNS servers." This is called a *referral*.

So what function do the *foo.example* NS records in the *foo.example* zone serve? After all, it's not as though, after it finds its way to the DNS servers authoritative for *foo.example*, a recursive DNS server needs *another* referral to those same DNS servers.

Actually, in many cases, when the authoritative *foo.example* DNS server responds to the recursive DNS server's query, it will include its list of NS records for *foo.example* in the response. That way, if the set of NS records in the *foo.example* zone differs from the set in the *example* zone, recursive DNS servers will still eventually learn and use the NS records in the authoritative zone data.

The set of NS records in the *foo.example* zone is also used by the zone's primary DNS server to determine where to send the NOTIFY messages that let the zone's secondary DNS servers know that the zone data has changed. (In fact, the secondaries might also use the NS records, if they send NOTIFY messages to other secondaries.)

Finally, the NS records also inform clients attempting to dynamically update *foo.example* domain names as to which DNS servers to try sending them to.

The SRV Record

The MX record provides a helpful level of abstraction between the domain name used in an email address and the mail servers that handle email for that destination. Similarly, the SRV record provides a layer of abstraction between domain names and the servers for, well, clients of just about any service.

SRV records are unique in that the domain names they are attached to have a prescribed format:

```
_service._protocol.domainname
```

The first label of the domain name is an underscore character followed by the symbolic name of a service, such as HTTP; the second label is an underscore followed by the symbolic name of a protocol, such as UDP, for the User Datagram Protocol or TCP, for the Transmission Control Protocol.[9] The domain name is any domain name. Clients interested in a particular service running over a particular protocol at a certain destination domain name would concatenate the service, protocol, and destination domain name to form a new domain name and then look up the SRV records for that domain name.

The underscore characters were chosen deliberately to minimize the chance that the domain names to which SRV records are attached would collide with existing domain names.

The RDATA of an SRV record has four fields:

Priority
    An unsigned, 16-bit integer that functions like the MX record's preference. Clients of the service would first try to connect to the target with the lowest priority

---

9 These symbolic names are often taken from STD 2, RFC 1700.

value; they would try targets with higher priority values only after trying all targets at lower values.

Weight

Another unsigned, 16-bit integer. When two or more targets share the same priority, clients are supposed to try to communicate with them in proportion to their associated weights. All of the weights of targets at the same priority are added; each target should receive a share of clients in proportion to its weight relative to the sum. So, two targets with the same priority and equal weights of 10 should each receive half of the clients. If one target has a weight of 200 and another has a weight of 100, the first target should receive two-thirds of the clients. (Of course, if a client can't successfully connect to the first target, it will try the other.)

Port

Yet another unsigned, 16-bit integer specifies the port on which the service runs. This is handy because it allows you to run services on any available port: if you're already running a web server on the HTTP port, TCP port 80, you can run an HTTP-based API server on another port and direct clients to it with an appropriate SRV record.

Target

This is the domain name of a server that offers the specified service. The domain name must own one or more A or AAAA records.

Examples 2-13 and 2-14 present two samples of SRV records.

Example 2-13. One example of SRV records

```
api.foo.example.  1m  IN  SRV  10  100  8080  api1.foo.example.
              # Connection to this server half the time
              1m  IN  SRV  10  100  8080  api2.bar.example.
              # ...and to this server half the time
```

Example 2-14. A more complicated example of SRV records

```
api.bar.example.  60  IN  SRV  100  200  80    api1.bar.example.
              # First try this server 2/3 of the time
              60  IN  SRV  100  100  8080  api2.bar.example.
              # ...or this server 1/3 of the time
              60  IN  SRV  200  100  8080  api1.foo.example.
              # And this server if neither of the others are available
```

The PTR Record

Mapping domain names to IP addresses is straightforward: you look up the A or AAAA record associated with the domain name. But what about mapping IP addresses back to domain names—something you might want to do for logging purposes or as a (weak) check of a client's identity? How do you do that?

To provide this function, DNS requires a special namespace—two, in fact. One is the domain *in-addr.arpa*, used to "reverse-map" IPv4 addresses to domain names. The other is *ip6.arpa*, used to reverse-map IPv6 addresses to domain names.

The labels under *in-addr.arpa* are the four octets of an IPv4 address, in reverse order: *octet4.octet3.octet2.octet1.in-addr.arpa*. Putting the most significant octet of the IPv4 address last makes sense, when you think about it: This way, the domain *32.128.in-addr.arpa* corresponds to the IPv4 network 128.32/16, which happens to be owned by U.C. Berkeley. The folks who run *in-addr.arpa* can then delegate *32.128.in-addr.arpa* to the folks at Berkeley responsible for the network.

So to reverse-map the IPv4 address 10.0.0.1 to a domain name, you look up PTR records for *1.0.0.10.in-addr.arpa*. The format of the PTR record is very simple: The RDATA is just a single domain name, the domain name that the corresponding IP address should map to, as shown in Example 2-15.

Example 2-15. A PTR record

```
1.0.0.10.in-addr.arpa.  1d  IN  PTR  host.foo.example.
```

IPv6 works in a similar fashion, though it requires longer domain names. To form the domain name that corresponds to an IPv6 address, you write all 32 of the hexadecimal digits of the IPv6 address in reverse order, each digit separated from the next by a dot, with ".ip6.arpa" appended to the end. So, for example, the IPv6 address 2001:db8:42:1:1 expands to 2001:0db8:0042:0001:0000:0000:0000:0001 and is then transformed into the domain name shown here:

```
1.0.0.0.0.0.0.0.0.0.0.0.0.0.0.0.1.0.0.0.2.4.0.0.8.b.d.0.1.0.0.2.ip6.arpa
```

As with IPv4, encoding the most significant hexadecimal digit of the address first makes delegation easier. And just as with IPv4, you attach a PTR record to the resulting domain name, as shown in Example 2-16.

Example 2-16. A PTR record for an IPv6 address

```
1.0.0.0.0.0.0.0.0.0.0.0.0.0.0.0.1.0.0.0.2.4.0.0.8.b.d.0.1.0.0.2.ip6.arpa.
  1d  IN  PTR  host-v6.foo.example.
```

The SOA Record

The SOA record provides summary information about a zone; consequently, there's only one SOA record per zone, and it must be attached to the domain name of the zone. The SOA record's RDATA format consists of seven fields:

- The MNAME field, which by convention is the domain name of the primary DNS server for the zone.
- The RNAME field, which by convention is the email address of a person or persons responsible for the zone. The format of the email address is a little peculiar: The "@" symbol in the email address is replaced with a dot ("."), so "cricket@foo.example" would become "cricket.foo.example."
- The zone's serial number, an unsigned 32-bit value.
- The zone's refresh interval, also an unsigned 32-bit value representing a duration. It can also be written as a scaled value, such as "1d" for one day or "30m" for 30 minutes.
- The zone's retry interval, likewise an unsigned 32-bit value representing a duration.
- The zone's expiration interval, an unsigned 32-bit value representing a duration.
- The zone's negative-caching TTL, an unsigned 32-bit value representing a duration.

Example 2-17 shows an SOA record.

Example 2-17. An SOA record

```
foo.example.  1d  IN  SOA  ns1.foo.example.  root.foo.example.  (
    2019050600   ; Serial number
    1h           ; Refresh interval
    15m          ; Retry interval
    7d           ; Expiration interval
    30m )        ; Default and negative-caching TTL
```

Note the "(" at the end of the first line of the record and matching ")" on the last line: This tells the DNS server to ignore carriage returns and newlines that occur between the parentheses. This syntax is legal for use with any record type, but you'll rarely see an SOA record that doesn't use it. The comments (beginning with ";" and extending to the end of the line) are also legal anywhere in a zone data file, but are particularly handy in the SOA record for DNS administrators who can't always remember what all seven RDATA fields mean.

The MNAME and RNAME fields are mostly read by people and ignored by software. For example, another DNS administrator having a problem with your zone or its DNS servers might look up your zone's SOA record to find your RNAME field and dash you off a quick question in email. The only exception is that some DNS software uses the MNAME field to help decide where to send dynamic updates for a zone, and secondary DNS servers for a zone typically don't send NOTIFY messages to the primary DNS server listed in MNAME.

The serial number and the refresh, retry, and expiration intervals are all related to zone transfers. The serial number is an indication of the version of a zone that a given authoritative DNS server holds. After each refresh interval, a secondary DNS server for a zone checks with its master DNS server (often the zone's primary) to see whether the master's serial number for the zone is higher than the secondary's. If the master has a higher serial number, the secondary requests a copy of the latest version of the zone with a zone transfer. If the check fails for some reason, the secondary keeps checking with the master at the retry interval (usually shorter than the refresh interval) until it successfully learns whether it needs a new version of the zone. And if the checks fail for the entire expiration interval (usually several refresh intervals), the secondary assumes its zone data is now out of date and expires the zone. After expiring the zone, a secondary will respond to queries in the zone with a Server Failed response code. This is illustrated in Figure 2-7.

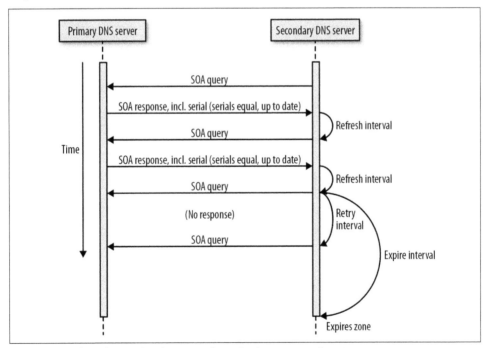

Figure 2-7. The relationship between the refresh, retry, and expire timers

The importance of the refresh interval has diminished somewhat since the advent of NOTIFY messages, which master DNS servers send to secondaries to inform them that a zone's data has changed. Still, it's a good idea to set a zone's refresh interval to a sensible value, no more than an hour or so, because the cost of the secondary's check of its master DNS server is so low: a single DNS query. The retry interval should usually be some fraction of the refresh interval; for instance, half or one-quarter. Because the consequences are fairly severe—responding to any queries in the zone with an error—the expiration interval should be long enough to give you time to notice that your secondary DNS server hasn't been able to communicate with its master and take corrective action. In practice, we usually set the expiration to at least one week.

The final field is the zone's negative-caching TTL. The negative-caching TTL specifies to other DNS servers how long they can cache negative responses from this zone's authoritative DNS servers. Negative responses include the following:

- No such domain name, indicating that the domain name in the query doesn't exist
- No such data, indicating that the domain name exists but there are no records of the type requested in the query

An authoritative DNS server for a zone includes the zone's SOA record in its negative responses so that the recursive DNS server that sent the query can determine how long it can cache the response.

Negative caching is very helpful in preventing your authoritative DNS servers from being bombarded with queries for the same, nonexistent domain name or record, but you shouldn't set the negative caching TTL too high, or it could hamper the resolution of brand-new domain names you add to your zone.

Whew! For "just enough" DNS theory, that's quite a bit. Let's just walk through a complete zone data file and call it a chapter.

An Annotated Zone Data File

Let's take a look at a complete (but hypothetical) zone data file. This should help give you a feeling for what to expect when reading others' zone data files or when writing your own. You might even decide that you like the formatting we use and follow our example.

Example 2-18 shows a zone data file for a zone we'll call *foo.example*.

Example 2-18. A zone data file for foo.example

```
@   1d   IN  SOA  ns1.foo.example.  root.foo.example.  (
    2019050800 ; Serial number
    1h          ; Refresh interval
    15m         ; Retry interval
    7d          ; Expiration interval
    10m         ; Negative-caching TTL
```

```
        IN  NS ns1.foo.example.
        IN  NS ns2.foo.example.
        IN  MX 0  mail.foo.example.
        IN  MX 10 mta.isp.net.
        IN  A 192.168.1.1
        IN  AAAA 2001:db8:42:1::1

www  5m IN  CNAME @

ns1     IN  A     192.168.1.53
        IN  AAAA  2001:db8:42:1::53
ns2     IN  A     192.168.2.53
        IN  AAAA  2001:db8:42:2::53

mail    IN  A     192.168.1.25
        IN  AAAA  2001:db8:42:1::25

_http._tcp.www   IN  SRV  0 0 80 foo.example.
_https._tcp.www  IN  SRV  0 0 443 foo.example.
```

The zone data file starts, as most do, with the SOA record, providing overall information about the zone. The SOA record is attached to @, the origin in the zone data file, which is *foo.example* by default.

The two NS records specify the authoritative DNS servers for *foo.example*, *ns1.foo.example*, and *ns2.foo.example*. These NS records are used mainly by *ns1* and *ns2* themselves, for determining where to send NOTIFY messages, and possibly by software trying to determine where to send dynamic updates to the *foo.example* zone. (There should be a matching set of NS records in the *example* zone that actually delegate *foo.example* to *ns1* and *ns2*.)

The MX records designate *mail.foo.example* and *mta.isp.net* as the mail exchangers for email addressed to *foo.example*. Given the preferences, *mta.isp.net* is likely a backup mail exchanger.

The A and AAAA records for *foo.example* point to the IPv4 and IPv6 addresses, respectively, of the *foo.example* web server. Attaching A and AAAA records directly to *foo.example* lets users type just "http://foo.example/" instead of "http://www.foo.example/", saving a few keystrokes.

The CNAME record creates an alias from *www.foo.example* to *foo.example*. Now users can type either "http://www.foo.example/" or "http://foo.example/" and get to the web server, and the DNS administrator only needs to edit one IPv4 or IPv6 address if an address changes. (The alias applies to protocols besides HTTP, of course, so users can also send mail to *someuser@www.foo.example*.)

The next six resource records give IPv4 and IPv6 addresses for *ns1.foo.example*, *ns2.foo.example*, and *mail.foo.example*. Clearly the network administrators of *foo.example* have done the work necessary to dual-stack their network—as should you!

The final two records are SRV records that direct SRV-savvy web clients to *foo.example*: the first SRV record applies to HTTP traffic, whereas the second applies to HTTP-S. Note that the target field contains *foo.example*, not *www.foo.example*: *www.foo.example* is an alias, so it shouldn't appear in the RDATA of an SRV record (or an MX record, for that matter).

Hopefully that gives you a good overview of how the Domain Name System works, including the roles of DNS servers and resolvers, the structure of the DNS namespace, and the syntax and semantics of various resource records. In the next chapter, we finally dive into what you've probably been waiting for: configuring your first CoreDNS-based DNS server!

## CHAPTER 3

Configuring CoreDNS

In Chapter 2, we covered basic DNS theory. That was to prepare you for the fun and excitement of configuring a CoreDNS server, which we do in this chapter.

CoreDNS is configured using a configuration file called the *Corefile*. The syntax of the Corefile follows that of the *Caddyfile*, given that CoreDNS actually uses the Caddy code to parse the configuration. First, though, we need to get CoreDNS set up.

Getting CoreDNS

Before configuring CoreDNS and writing your first *Corefile*, you need a copy of the *coredns* executable for your OS. The easiest way to find executables of the latest version of CoreDNS for your OS is to start at the coredns.io website (*https://coredns.io*). There, you'll see a prominent button labeled Download, as shown in Figure 3-1.

Figure 3-1. The Download button on coredns.io

Clicking Download takes you directly to the part of the CoreDNS GitHub repository where you can download the *coredns* executable, as illustrated in Figure 3-2.

Figure 3-2. The CoreDNS GitHub repository

If you'd prefer to build your own copy of *coredns*, you can download the source code (zip, tar, or GZIP, according to your preference) from one of the two links at the bottom of the page.[1] Otherwise, choose the file appropriate for the OS you're running and the processor it's running on. Here's a guide:

- "Darwin" is MacOS X
- There are builds of CoreDNS for many different processors, including AMD, ARM, 64-bit ARM, PowerPC, and IBM's S/390

---

1 If you're wondering why you'd want to do that, or how to do it, see Chapter 9.

- Windows is... well, Microsoft Windows

After you've downloaded the file, download the accompanying checksum file, which has the same name as the file you've downloaded with *.sha256* appended. Run your favorite checksum program against the first file to generate its SHA-256 checksum. For example, on MacOS X, you could run the following:

```
% shasum -a 256 coredns_1.4.0_darwin_amd64.tgz
```

On Linux operating systems, you might use the *sha256sum* program.

Compare the result to the contents of the *.sha256* file and make sure they match. If not, your download might have been corrupted.

After you've verified that the file downloaded correctly, you can extract the *coredns* executable. For tar and gzip files, you can use the following:

```
% tar -zxvf coredns_1.4.0_darwin_amd64.tgz
x coredns
```

The *coredns* executable extracts into the current working directory; you can move it wherever you'd like. You can make sure it works by running it with the -version command-line option; it should print something like the following:

```
% coredns -version
CoreDNS-1.4.0
darwin/amd64, go1.12, 8dcc7fc
```

That looks reasonable, so we can move on to configuring CoreDNS.

CoreDNS Command-Line Options

Now that you have a working copy of CoreDNS, let's look at the command-line options it supports:

-conf
Specifies the path to CoreDNS's configuration file. The default is *Corefile* in core dns's working directory.

-cpu
Specifies the maximum CPU percentage coredns is allowed to use. The default is 100%. You can specify the percentage either as an integer (e.g., "50") or as a percentage (e.g., "50%").

 This option has been deprecated, and might not be supported in newer versions of CoreDNS.

`-dns.port`

Specifies the port on which `coredns` should listen for queries. By default, it's 53, the standard DNS port.

`-help`

Displays `coredns`'s usage, including these options.

`-pidfile`

Specifies the path to the file to which `coredns` should write its process ID. There's no default.

`-plugins`

Displays the list of plug-ins compiled into the `coredns` executable. Unless you built `coredns` yourself, this includes all "in-tree" plug-ins.

`-quiet`

Suppresses initialization output.

`-version`

Prints the `coredns` version.

 Note that there are no options for controlling where logging is sent. That's a deliberate choice on the part of the developers: CoreDNS logs to standard output by default, but leaves the management of logs to other software.

For now, we'll run the `coredns` executable with no or minimal options. Let's talk about the *Corefile* next.

Corefile Syntax

Before writing our first *Corefile*, we need to go over its syntax and structure. *Corefiles* consist of one or more *entries*, which themselves comprise *labels* and *definitions*. That looks something like Example 3-1.

Example 3-1. Sample Corefile

```
# What follows is called an "entry"
label {
    definition
}
```

Unless a *Corefile* consists of only one entry, the entries' definitions must be enclosed in curly braces to show CoreDNS the bounds of each entry. The opening curly brace

({) must appear at the end of the line that begins with the label; the closing curly brace (}) must appear alone on a line. The text within the curly braces is referred to as a *block*.

Stylistically, definitions are usually indented with tabs, though that's not required. Comments begin with # and extend to the end of the line.

Sometimes, an entry will begin with multiple labels, in which case the labels can be separated by spaces, as shown in Example 3-2.

Example 3-2. Another sample Corefile

```
label1 label2 {
    definition
}
```

If the list of labels is so long that it spans multiple lines, the last label on all but the last line must end in a comma, as demonstrated in Example 3-3.

Example 3-3. A lengthy list of labels

```
label1, label2,
label3, label4,
label5 {
    definition
}
```

(You could use spaces between the labels on the same line and a comma just at the end, but that's just weird.)

Definitions are made up of *directives* and optional *arguments*. Each line of the definition begins with a directive, followed by zero or more arguments, like that shown in Example 3-4.

Example 3-4. Labels, directives, and arguments

```
label {
    directive1 arg1 arg2
    directive2
}
```

If the list of arguments spans multiple lines, you must enclose those lines using curly braces, with the opening curly brace at the end of the directive's first line and the closing curly brace along on the last line, as illustrated in Example 3-5.

Example 3-5. A multiple-line argument

```
label {
    directive1 arg1 arg2
    directive2 {
        arg3
        arg4
    }
}
```

As Example 3-6 shows, *subdirectives* can appear within a directive, as long as they begin the line. And those subdirectives can have arguments of their own.

Example 3-6. Subdirectives and arguments

```
label {
    directive1 arg1 arg2
    directive2 {
        subdirective arg3 arg4
        arg5
    }
}
```

The subdirectives can't begin a new curly-brace-delimited block, which is a small mercy.

Next, let's look at environment variables, a convenient way of substituting text into the *Corefile*.

Environment Variables

Corefiles can also contain references to *environment variables*, which expand into their values to become labels, directives, or arguments, or parts of those. The name of the environment variable must be enclosed in curly braces, as demonstrated in Example 3-7.

Example 3-7. Using environment variables in Corefiles

```
label_{$ENV_VAR_1} {
    directive {$ENV_VAR_2}
}
```

You can also use the Windows environment variable syntax, %ENV_VAR%, but who does that?

Reusable Snippets

If you're going to reuse a section of configuration several times in a *Corefile*, you can define it as a *reusable snippet* (yes, that's the official name) by providing a name for the snippet in parentheses and enclosing the snippet itself in curly braces, as presented in Example 3-8.

Example 3-8. A reusable snippet

```
(snippet1) {
    label1 {
        directive1 arg1
        directive2 arg2 arg3
    }
}
```

Then, to insert the snippet into another part of the *Corefile*, you use the `import` directive with the name of the snippet (without parentheses), as shown here:

```
import snippet1
```

Import

Besides importing snippets, you can use the `import` directive to import files. `import` can take a pathname or a Glob pattern as an argument (in addition to a reference to a snippet, which we've already seen), as illustrated in Example 3-9.

Example 3-9. Importing a file and all the files in a directory

```
import common.conf
import config/*.conf
```

Server Blocks

For CoreDNS, the most common entry is called a *server block*. A server block defines a *server* within CoreDNS, a configuration that determines how queries for particular domain names, received on particular ports and over particular protocols, are processed. In its simplest form, the server block's label is just the domain name of a domain that matches some set of queries, as shown in Example 3-10.

Example 3-10. foo.example server block

```
foo.example {
    # directives go here
}
```

This server block would apply to all queries for domain names that end in `foo.exam`
`ple` (unless there were a more specific server block that applied to, say, `bar.foo.exam`
`ple`). To specify a server block that will apply to all queries, use the root as the label,
as illustrated in Example 3-11.

Example 3-11. Root server block

```
. {
    # directives go here
}
```

If a set of directives are common to multiple domains, remember that you can use a
list of labels, as shown in Example 3-12.

Example 3-12. A server block for multiple domains

```
foo.example bar.example {
    # directives go here
}
```

By default, CoreDNS listens on User Datagram Protocol (UDP) port 53 and Transmission Control Protocol (TCP) port 53, the standard DNS ports. To configure a
server to listen on a nondefault port, add a colon (`:`) after the domain name label and
the port number, as listed in Example 3-13.

Example 3-13. Listening on a nondefault port

```
.:1053 {
    # directives go here
}
```

Finally, by default, CoreDNS speaks plain-old DNS. But CoreDNS can also speak
DNS over Transport Layer Security (TLS), aka DoT, and DNS over general-purpose
Remote Procedure Call (gRPC). To configure CoreDNS to speak DoT or DNS over
gRPC for certain domains or over certain ports, use the prefixes `tls://` or `grpc://`,
respectively, before the domain name label, as demonstrated in Example 3-14.

Example 3-14. Using protocol prefixes

```
tls://foo.example {
    # directives go here
}

grpc://bar.example {
    # directives go here
}
```

Query Processing

The way CoreDNS processes queries is somewhat unique among DNS servers. It resembles, if anything, the way BIND DNS servers handle multiple views, if you're familiar with that sort of thing.

When CoreDNS receives a query, it examines the *Corefile* to find an applicable server block. For a server block to apply to a given query, the protocol (TLS, gRPC, or plain-vanilla DNS) port on which the query was received and domain name in the query must match the label. In the event that the domain name in the query matches multiple labels, the longest (i.e., most specific) match wins. For example, let's consider the Corefile in Example 3-15.

Example 3-15. A sample Corefile

```
# First entry
foo.example {
    # directive1
}

# Second entry
tls://foo.example {
    # directive2
}

# Third entry
bar.example {
    # directive3
}

# Fourth entry
bar.example:1053 {
    # directive4
}

# Fifth entry
. {
    # directive5
    # directive6
}
```

A query received on port 53 (the standard DNS port) for *www.foo.example* would match the first entry, thus directive1 would apply. A query received over TLS on the default DNS over TLS port (853) for *www.foo.example*, on the other hand, would match the second entry, thus directive2 would apply. A query for MX records for *bar.example* received on port 53 would match the third entry, whereas if it were received on port 1053, it would match the fourth entry. And finally, queries received on port 53 over plain-vanilla DNS about domain names that don't end in *foo.example* or *bar.example* would match the fifth entry and have `directive5` and `directive6` applied.

That's it for syntax! Let's talk about plug-ins, which is where all the work is done.

Plug-ins

What are the configuration directives that control how CoreDNS responds to queries? In CoreDNS, they're *plug-ins*, software modules that implement DNS functionality.

In this section, we cover seven basic plug-ins, enough to set up a working DNS server that's authoritative for a few zones, uses forwarders, and caches responses from forwarders. In later chapters, we cover more advanced plug-ins, including those that interface with Kubernetes.

Here's a list of the plug-ins covered in this section and their functions:

Root
: Configures the working directory for CoreDNS.

File
: Configures CoreDNS as a primary DNS server for a zone, loading zone data from a file.

Secondary
: Configures CoreDNS as a secondary DNS server for a zone, loading zone data from a master DNS server.

Forward
: Configures CoreDNS to forward queries to one or more forwarders.

Cache
: Configures CoreDNS to cache responses to queries.

Errors
: Configures CoreDNS to log errors.

Log
: Configures CoreDNS to log each query it receives, à la BIND's query logging.

Without further ado, the root plug-in.

Root

The root plug-in specifies CoreDNS's current working directory, which is where CoreDNS expects to find zone data files, among other things.

Example 3-16 shows the syntax for the root plug-in.

Example 3-16. The root plug-in

```
. {
    root /etc/coredns/zones
}
```

Obviously, CoreDNS needs to be able to read files in this directory. For CoreDNS to actually read a file, we need the file plug-in.

File

The file plug-in configures the server as the primary DNS server for the zone or zones in the server block or for a specified list of zones. Because a primary DNS server loads data that describes zones from zone data files, file takes the name of a zone data file as an argument. Example 3-17 presents the complete syntax of the file plug-in.

Example 3-17. Syntax of the file plug-in

```
file DBFILE [ZONES...] {
    transfer to ADDRESS...
    reload DURATION
}
```

If ZONES is omitted, the file will be read as the zone data file for the zone(s) specified in the server block. If specified, ZONES will override the zone(s) specified in the server block. The ZONES must, however, fall within the zone(s) specified in the server block, or the server won't receive queries for those zones. If multiple zones share a single zone data file, that zone data file must contain relative domain names. For more information on this, see Chapter 4.

The `transfer` subdirective enables "outbound" transfers of the zone (from this DNS server to secondary DNS servers). The arguments can be IPv4 addresses, IPv6 addresses, IPv4 or IPv6 networks in Classless Inter-Domain Routing (CIDR) notation, or the wildcard, *, meaning "all IPv4 and IPv6 addresses." For any arguments that are individual IPv4 or IPv6 addresses, CoreDNS will notify those DNS servers of any changes to the zone.[2] You can use multiple `transfer from` subdirectives in a single `file` directive.

The `reload` subdirective instructs CoreDNS to check the zone data file periodically to see whether the zone's start of authority (SOA) record's serial number has incremented. If it has, CoreDNS will reload the zone. The argument specifies the amount of time between checks; use a integer followed by "s" for seconds, "m" for minutes, or "h" for hours. Setting `reload` to 0 disables the periodic checking.

Example 3-18 provides some samples of the `file` plug-in:

Example 3-18. The file plug-in

```
foo.example {
    file db.foo.example {
        transfer to 10.0.0.1
    }
}

. {
    file db.template.example bar.example baz.example {
        transfer to *
    }
}
```

That's how you set up a simple primary DNS server. How about a secondary next?

Secondary

The `secondary` plug-in configures CoreDNS as a secondary DNS server for one or more zones. Specifying the zones works the same way it does with the `file` plug-in: It's either inherited from the server block or specified as arguments to the directive.

---

2 Using DNS NOTIFY messages.

Example 3-19 shows the syntax of the secondary plug-in.

Example 3-19. The secondary plug-in

```
secondary [ZONES...] {
    transfer from ADDRESS
    transfer to ADDRESS
}
```

The transfer from subdirective specifies the IPv4 or IPv6 address of the master DNS server from which to transfer this zone. If you'd like CoreDNS to try more than one master DNS server, you can use multiple transfer from subdirectives.

The transfer to subdirective works exactly as it does in the file plug-in, determining which secondary DNS servers are allowed to transfer this zone from CoreDNS.

CoreDNS servers, notably, do not store zone data for secondary zones in a backup zone data file. This means that each time CoreDNS restarts, it must transfer all secondary zones from their master DNS servers. CoreDNS also doesn't support incremental zone transfers, or IXFRs, so those transfers contain the entire contents of the zones.

Example 3-20 offers some examples of the secondary plug-in in use.

Example 3-20. The secondary plug-in

```
foo.example {
    secondary {
        transfer from 10.0.0.1
        transfer from 10.0.1.1
    }
}

. {
    secondary bar.example {
        transfer from 10.0.0.1
        transfer to *
    }
}
```

Now you have all the plug-ins that you need to configure an authoritative DNS server. Next, let's look at how to configure a forwarder.

Forward

The `forward` plug-in configures CoreDNS to use a forwarder, which was described in Chapter 2. Example 3-21 shows basic syntax for `forward`.

Example 3-21. Syntax of the forward plug-in

```
forward FROM TO...
```

If a query matches the domain name in `FROM` (i.e., if it's within the domain, which is to say it ends in that domain name), CoreDNS forwards the query to the DNS servers specified as forwarders by `TO`. If a forwarder is specified as an IP address, plain-vanilla DNS is used to forward the query. The forwarder can optionally be specified with a protocol prefix, somewhat like the labels for entries. The prefix `tls://` indicates a forwarder that accepts DNS queries over TLS, whereas `dns://` indicates a traditional DNS forwarder. You can configure up to 15 forwarders.

Example 3-22 displays samples of the `forward` plug-in.

Example 3-22. The forward plug-in

```
# Forward queries for foo.example to 10.0.0.1
foo.example {
    forward foo.example 10.0.0.1
}

# Forward all other queries to Google Public DNS over TLS
. {
    forward . tls://8.8.8.8 tls://8.8.4.4
}
```

CoreDNS uses an in-band mechanism to check the health of the forwarders, sending each forwarder a recursive query for the NS records for the root every half second. This probe is sent over the transport specified for the forwarder, so in Example 3-22, over plain-vanilla DNS to 10.0.0.1, and using DoT for 8.8.8.8 and 8.8.4.4. As long as a forwarder responds, even with a negative response such as NXDOMAIN or a DNS error such as SERVFAIL, CoreDNS counts it as healthy. If a forwarder fails to respond or responds with an empty reply twice in a row, it's marked unhealthy. If for whatever reason *all* of the forwarders appear unhealthy, CoreDNS assumes that the health-checking mechanism itself has failed and will query a randomly chosen forwarder.

The `forward` plug-in provides control over health checking and more with its extended syntax, as presented in Example 3-23.

Example 3-23. Syntax of the forward plug-in

```
forward FROM TO... {
    except IGNORED_NAMES...
    force_tcp
    prefer_udp
    expire DURATION
    max_fails INTEGER
    health_check DURATION
    policy random|round_robin|sequential
    tls CERT KEY CA
    tls_servername NAME

}
```

The except subdirective allows you to specify subdomains of the domain specified in FROM that shouldn't be forwarded.

Usually, CoreDNS will use the same protocol to forward a query over which it receives the query; in other words, if it receives a query over UDP, CoreDNS will forward via UDP, whereas if it receives a query over TCP, it will forward using TCP. force_tcp instructs CoreDNS to forward queries to the forwarders via TCP even if they arrived over UDP, whereas prefer_udp directs CoreDNS to forward via UDP, even if those queries arrived over TCP.[3] Forcing queries to use TCP might improve resistance to cache poisoning attacks, for instance, or make it easier to craft firewall rules to permit just that traffic.

max_fails is the number of consecutive health checks that must fail before CoreDNS considers a forwarder down. The default is 2; configuring max_fails to 0 instructs CoreDNS to never mark a forwarder down. health_check configures the period between sending health checks to forwarders; by default, it's 0.5 seconds.

For efficiency, CoreDNS will reuse TCP and TLS connections to forwarders. The expire subdirective controls how long CoreDNS will wait before expiring a cached connection. The default is 10 seconds.

The policy subdirective controls the order in which multiple forwarders are queried:

- random chooses a forwarder at random.
- round_robin chooses the first forwarder to query in roundrobin fashion. For example, if the forwarders are listed in the order 10.0.0.1, 10.0.1.1, and 10.0.2.1, for the first query, CoreDNS will first forward to 10.0.0.1, falling back to 10.0.1.1 if there's no response. For the next query, CoreDNS will first forward to 10.0.1.1 and then fall back to 10.0.2.1, if necessary. Unhealthy forwarders are skipped.

---

3 Of course, if the forwarded UDP query elicits a truncated response, CoreDNS will retry over TCP.

- sequential always uses the forwarders in the order in which they're listed. For example, if the forwarders are listed in the order 10.0.0.1, 10.0.1.1, and 10.0.2.1, for each query, CoreDNS will first forward to 10.0.0.1, then to 10.0.1.1, and then to 10.0.2.1. Again, unhealthy forwarders are skipped.

It wouldn't do to ask forwarders to resolve domain names for CoreDNS and then immediately forget the answer, would it? Thankfully, CoreDNS can cache responses.

Cache

The cache plug-in controls (wait for it...) caching. Each server can have its own cache configuration, which you configure in its server block. Example 3-24 illustrates the basic syntax of the cache plug-in.

Example 3-24. Syntax of the cache plug-in

```
cache [TTL] [ZONES...]
```

The simple presence of the cache plug-in instructs CoreDNS to cache data from all sources (including other DNS servers and backends such as Kubernetes) for up to one hour, or 3,600 seconds. Negative responses are cached for a maximum of 1,800 seconds. CoreDNS will trim the time-to-live (TTL) value of records and negative responses with longer TTLs to the maximum before caching them. TTL allows configuration of a different maximum TTL, in seconds.

Specifying the zones to which the cache applies works the same way it does with the file plug-in: It's either inherited from the server block or specified as arguments to the directive.

Example 3-25 provides some examples of the cache plug-in in use.

Example 3-25. The cache plug-in

```
# Cache data about foo.example received from 10.0.0.1 for up to 600s
foo.example {
    forward . 10.0.0.1
    cache 600
}

# Cache data about bar.example received from 8.8.8.8 or 8.8.4.4
. {
    forward . 8.8.8.8 8.8.4.4
    cache 3600 bar.example
}
```

cache supports three optional subdirectives, as shown in Example 3-26, if you need more control over caching.

Example 3-26. Full syntax of the cache plug-in

```
cache [TTL] [ZONES...] {
    success CAPACITY [TTL] [MINTTL]
    denial CAPACITY [TTL] [MINTTL]
    prefetch AMOUNT [DURATION] [PERCENTAGE%]
}
```

The success subdirective gives you finer-grained control over "positive" caching (i.e., caching of records). CAPACITY is the maximum number of packets CoreDNS will cache before randomly evicting old packets from the cache. The default CAPACITY is 9,984 packets, and the minimum configurable CAPACITY is 1,024. CAPACITY *should* be an integer evenly divisible by 256. TTL overrides the cache's maximum TTL, and MINTTL overrides the cache's minimum TTL, which by default is 5 seconds.

The denial subdirective provides the same sort of control as success, but for "negative" caching (caching of negative responses such as "No such domain name"). Again, when CAPACITY is reached, old entries are randomly evicted from the cache.

Finally, prefetch allows you to control *prefetching* of cached data. Some cached data is so frequently looked up that it makes sense for CoreDNS to "refresh" it before it ages out of the cache by looking it up again; this is called "prefetching." By default, prefetching is off. If you enable it with the prefetch subdirective, if AMOUNT queries are received for a given cached answer without a gap of DURATION between them, CoreDNS will try to look up the answer again after the TTL of the cached answer reaches a PERCENTAGE of its original value. DURATION is 1m (one minute) by default, and PERCENTAGE is 10%. Note that the value for PERCENTAGE must be an integer followed by the % sign.

We cover error messages produced by CoreDNS in the next section.

Errors

The errors plug-in instructs CoreDNS to log errors encountered during query processing within a server block. Errors are sent to standard output. The basic syntax is shown in Example 3-27.

Example 3-27. Syntax of the errors plug-in

```
errors
```

Example 3-28 shows how this plug-in works.

Example 3-28. The errors plug-in

```
foo.example {
    file db.foo.example
    errors
}

. {
    forward . 8.8.8.8 8.8.4.4
    cache 3600
    errors
}
```

For more control over how and when errors are logged, there's a `consolidate` subdirective, as shown in Example 3-29.

Example 3-29. Full syntax of the errors plug-in

```
errors {
    consolidate DURATION REGEXP
}
```

When specified, `consolidate` causes CoreDNS to collect as many error messages as match the regular expression `REGEXP` in `DURATION` and log a summary message instead. To consolidate more than one error message, use multiple `consolidate` subdirectives. Take a look at the `errors` plug-in given in Example 3-30.

Example 3-30. Sample errors plug-in

```
. {
    forward . 8.8.8.8 8.8.4.4
    cache 3600
    errors {
        consolidate 5m ".* timeout$"
        consolidate 30s "^Failed to .+"
    }
}
```

This would cause CoreDNS to consolidate timeout and failure messages every 5 minutes and 30 seconds, respectively, producing consolidated messages that look like this:

```
3 errors like '^Failed to .+' occurred in last 30s
```

We recommend that you use the anchors ^ or $ in the regular expression to improve performance.

Sometimes, in addition to errors, you want to know what CoreDNS is up to, like which queries it's processing. That's the job of the log plug-in.

Log

The log plug-in instructs CoreDNS to dump information about all queries (and some parts of the reply) to standard output. Like the errors plug-in, the basic format of the log plug-in is very simple, as you can see in Example 3-31.

Example 3-31. The log plug-in

```
log
```

Without arguments, this causes CoreDNS to write a query log entry to standard output for all requests received. Example 3-32 presents a sample.

Example 3-32. Sample query log output

```
2019-02-28T19:10:07.547Z [INFO] [::1]:50759 - 29008 "A IN foo.example. udp 41 false
 4096" NOERROR qr,rd,ra,ad 68 0.037990251s
```

The log plug-in does offer more control over both what is logged and the format in which it is logged. Example 3-33 shows the expanded syntax.

Example 3-33. Syntax of the log plug-in

```
log [NAMES...] [FORMAT]
```

NAMES specifies the domain names that should be logged. All domain names in the specified domain (i.e., all those that end in the specified domain name) are logged.

FORMAT specifies the format of the log messages. Example 3-34 shows the default, but CoreDNS also allows you to specify which fields in the query to log:

{type}
> The query's type.

{name}
> The domain name in the query.

{class}
> The class of the query.

{proto}
> The protocol over which the query was received (UDP or TCP).

`{remote}`
> The IP address from which the query was received. IPv6 addresses are enclosed in brackets (e.g., `[::1]`).

`{local}`
> The IP address on the server on which the query was received. Again, IPv6 addresses appear in brackets.

`{size}`
> The size of the query, in bytes.

`{port}`
> The port from which the query was received.

`{duration}`
> The "duration" of the response (how long it took to process the query and respond).

`{rcode}`
> The response code (RCODE) of the response.

`{rsize}`
> The raw, uncompressed size of the response.

`{>rflags}`
> Flags set in the header of the response.

`{>bufsize}`
> The `EDNS0` buffer size advertised in the query.

`{>do}`
> Whether the DNSSEC OK (DO) but was set in the query.

`{>id}`
> The query ID.

`{>opcode}`
> The query OPCODE.

`{common}`
> The Common Log Format (the default).

`{combined}`
> The Common Log Format plus the query opcode (`{>opcode}`).

Example 3-34 displays the default log format, in terms of these fields.

Example 3-34. The Common Log Format

```
{remote}:{port} - {>id} "{type} {class} {name} {proto} {size} {>do} {>bufsize}"
 {rcode} {>rflags} {rsize} {duration}
```

You can even control the classes of responses that are logged. CoreDNS recognizes four classes:

success
> Includes all successful responses

denial
> Includes all negative responses (no such domain name and no data)

error
> Includes the server failed, not implemented, format error, and refused errors

all
> Includes all three of the other classes

Example 3-35 lists the syntax for specifying classes.

Example 3-35. Full syntax of the log plug-in

```
log [NAMES...] [FORMAT] {
    class [CLASSES...]
}
```

Example 3-36 presents a few samples of the log plug-in.

Example 3-36. The log plug-in

```
foo.example {
    file db.foo.example
    errors
    log {
        class success denial
    }
}

bar.example {
    file db.bar.example
    errors
    log
}

# Log clients who do lookups in the defunct baz.example domain
```

```
. {
    forward . 8.8.8.8 8.8.4.4
    errors
    log baz.example "Client: {remote}, query name: {name}"
}
```

That should be enough about plug-ins to get you started. Now let's cover configuration options common to multiple plug-ins.

Common Configuration Options

There are a few common configuration options that you will see in several different plug-ins. The developers of CoreDNS make a special effort to ensure that plug-in options that perform the same actions work in a consistent way across plug-ins.

We begin with `fallthrough`, which you use to control when query processing is passed from one plug-in to another, and then we cover `tls`, which you use to configure client-side TLS.

fallthrough

Normally (without this option), when a plug-in has been given authority for a zone, it provides a response for any query in that zone. If the requested name does not exist, it will return the DNS response code NXDOMAIN. If the name exists but there is no data of the specified type, it will return an empty answer (also known as NODATA, although that is not a real response code). In some cases, however, we might want to give another plug-in a chance to answer the query. That is what the `fallthrough` option does.

This option appears in several plug-ins and can be added to others as needed.

tls

The `tls` option enables the configuration of client-side TLS certificates. This is so that CoreDNS can initiate secure communications with external entities such as Kubernetes. Do not confuse this with the `tls` *plug-in*, which you use to configure the CoreDNS *server's* TLS certificates. This option can have zero to three arguments:

`tls`

> Without any parameters, this means that the TLS client should verify the server's client certificate using the standard certificate authorities installed on the system.

`tls CERT-FILE KEY-FILE`

> This will present the provided client certificate to the server. The server certificate will be verified using the standard certificate authorities (CAs) installed on the system.

```
tls CERT-FILE KEY-FILE CA-FILE
```
This will present the provided client certificate to the server. The server certificate will be verified using the certificate in the CA-FILE.

transfer to

The `transfer to` subdirective enables "outbound" transfers of the zone (from this DNS server to secondary DNS servers). The arguments can be IPv4 addresses, IPv6 addresses, IPv4 or IPv6 networks in CIDR notation, or the wildcard, *, meaning "all IPv4 and IPv6 addresses." For any arguments that are individual IPv4 or IPv6 addresses, CoreDNS will notify those DNS servers of any changes to the zone.

Now it's time to put some plug-ins together into real-world configurations!

Sample DNS Server Configurations

Even these few plug-ins can be combined into *Corefiles* that configure CoreDNS to perform useful functions. Let's go through three *Corefiles*, representing the configurations of a caching-only DNS server, a primary DNS server, and a secondary DNS server.

Caching-Only DNS Server

Example 3-37 presents a *Corefile* for a caching-only DNS server. Caching-only DNS servers can look up any domain name but aren't authoritative for any zones. They're useful on busy servers because they provide a local cache of frequently looked-up resource records.

The configuration of a caching-only DNS server is fairly straightforward: we use a single entry for the root with the `forward` plug-in to tell CoreDNS which forwarders to use (because it can't yet do recursion by itself) and the `cache` plug-in to direct CoreDNS to cache the responses it receives. We also use the `errors` and `logs` plug-ins to help us diagnose problems later.

Example 3-37. Corefile for a caching-only DNS server

```
. {
    forward . 8.8.8.8 8.8.4.4
    cache
    errors
    log
}
```

Primary DNS Server

You might use a simple primary DNS server to host one or a few zones. The Corefile for a primary DNS server is a little more complicated than that for a caching-only DNS server, but not much. We'll use an entry for *foo.example*, the zone this DNS server will be primary for, with the root plug-in to specify to CoreDNS which directory we'll put our zone data files in. (If we didn't, we'd need to specify the full pathname to the zone data file, which for a single primary zone isn't a big deal.) Then, we'll use the file plug-in to configure the DNS server as the primary for the zone and to specify the name of the zone data file, *db.foo.example*. We'll also use the errors and log plug-ins to alert us if there are problems loading the zone and to log queries we receive in *foo.example*, respectively.

Some DNS servers serve double-duty as both authoritative and recursive DNS servers. If this is one of those, we'll also need an entry like the one shown in Example 3-38, specifying forwarders and the cache plug-in.

Example 3-38. Corefile for a primary DNS server

```
foo.example {
    root /etc/coredns/zones
     # Don't forget to tell CoreDNS which directory to look in!
    file db.foo.example
    errors
    log
}

# If you want your DNS server to handle recursive queries, too,
# you'll need an entry like the following.  If it's authoritative-
# only, omit it.

. {
    forward 8.8.8.8 8.8.4.4
    cache
    errors
    log
}
```

Secondary DNS Server

A secondary DNS server provides authoritative answers to queries in the zones for which it's authoritative, but those zones are managed elsewhere (on a different DNS server). They're useful because they provide a local source of answers to queries in the secondary zones, obviating the need to send those queries to a different DNS server.

As Example 3-39 demonstrates, the *Corefile* for a secondary DNS server is like the one for a primary DNS server but adds an entry for the secondary zone, *bar.example*, with the required `transfer from` subdirective to specify the IP address of the master DNS server. This time, because we're going to use the `errors` and `log` plug-ins repeatedly, we define a reusable snippet called *logerrors* that will substitute for both of them.

Example 3-39. Corefile for a secondary DNS server

```
(logerrors) {
    errors
    log
}

bar.example {
    transfer from 10.0.0.1
    import logerrors
}

# A given DNS server can, of course, be secondary for some zones
# and primary for others...

foo.example {
    file db.foo.example
    root /etc/coredns/zones
    import logerrors
}

# And again, if you want your DNS server to handle recursive
# queries

. {
    forward 8.8.8.8 8.8.4.4
    cache
    import logerrors
}
```

Of course, those are just a few of the possible configurations of DNS servers you can implement with CoreDNS. In upcoming chapters, we cover many more.

This chapter should have given you a good overall understanding of how to configure CoreDNS, including the syntax of the *Corefile* and how to use seven basic plug-ins to perform useful functions. In Chapter 4, we cover how to manage and serve zone data with CoreDNS.

Managing Zone Data

With traditional DNS servers, such as BIND, administrators usually manage primary zone data as files. More recently, DNS servers have begun to support loading primary zone data from other sources, such as databases.

CoreDNS supports a variety of methods to manage zone data. Some will be very familiar to DNS administrators, like zone data files; others are more modern, such as using Git; whereas some are downright retro (host tables, anyone?). In this chapter, we cover all of them.

Together, these options provide administrators with flexibility and, in some cases, advanced functionality in the mechanism they use to manage zone data. Host tables, for example, provide a simple way to add name-to-address and address-to-name mappings without the overhead of creating and maintaining an entire zone data file. Git, on the other hand, provides distributed version-control capabilities.

Let's begin with the file plug-in, which supports zone data files. We actually covered this in Chapter 3, but we go through it in more detail here.

The file Plug-in

For an administrator with experience managing zone data files, the file plug-in is probably the most familiar mechanism CoreDNS offers. file configures CoreDNS as the primary DNS server for one or more zones. In its simplest form, the file plug-in takes the syntax shown in Example 4-1.

Example 4-1. Simple file plug-in syntax

```
file DBFILE [ZONES...]
```

DBFILE is a zone data file containing resource records. You can specify DBFILE as a full pathname or as a relative pathname; relative pathnames are interpreted relative to any path set with the root directive.

ZONES is an optional list of one or more zones described by the resource records in DBFILE. If ZONES is omitted, CoreDNS uses the zones from the configuration block.

Example 4-2 presents a simple example of a file plug-in, and Example 4-3 shows the zone data file it refers to.

Example 4-2. Simple example of a file plug-in

```
foo.example {
    file db.foo.example
}
```

Example 4-3. db.foo.example

```
@   3600   IN   SOA   ns1.foo.example.   root.foo.example.   (
    2019041900
    3600
    600
    604800
    600 )
    3600   IN   NS   ns1.foo.example.
    3600   IN   NS   ns2.foo.example.

ns1      IN   A   10.0.0.53
         IN   AAAA   2001:db8:42:1::53
ns2      IN   A   10.0.1.53
         IN   AAAA   2001:db8:42:2::53
www      IN   A   10.0.0.1
         IN   AAAA   2001:db8:42:1:1
```

Because the resource records in the db.foo.example zone data file are all attached to relative domain names (e.g., ns1 and www rather than dot-terminated fully qualified domain names), the file can be loaded to describe multiple zones, as shown in Example 4-4.

Example 4-4. Using a single zone data file for multiple zones

```
. {
    file db.foo.example foo.example bar.example
}
```

This assumes that you want the contents of *foo.example* and *bar.example* to be identical, of course—for example, that you want both *www.foo.example* and *www.bar.example* to map to the IPv4 address 10.0.0.1.

The `file` plug-in also supports a more extensive syntax that allows you to specify which DNS servers are allowed to transfer the zone(s) and how frequently to check the zone data file for changes, as demonstrated in Example 4-5.

Example 4-5. More detailed syntax of the file plug-in

```
file DBFILE [ZONES... ] {
    transfer to ADDRESS...
    reload DURATION
    upstream [ADDRESS...]
}
```

Without a `transfer` directive, CoreDNS will not allow zone transfers of the zone or zones described by the `file` plug-in. To send NOTIFY messages to a particular secondary DNS server as well as to allow zone transfers to that secondary, specify the secondary's IP address. For multiple secondaries, you can list their IP addresses in a single `transfer` directive or use multiple directives. You can also specify a network in Classless Inter-Domain Routing (CIDR) notation to allow zone transfers from any IP address on that network, or * to allow zone transfers from anywhere, as presented in Example 4-6.

Example 4-6. Detailed example of the file plug-in

```
foo.example {
    file db.foo.example {
        transfer to 10.0.1.53
        transfer to *
    }
}
```

`reload` allows you to specify how frequently CoreDNS checks the zone data file to determine whether the serial number in the start of authority (SOA) record has changed. When CoreDNS detects a new serial number, it reloads the file (as one or more zones) and sends NOTIFY messages to secondary DNS servers designated in `transfer` directives. The default `reload` is one minute; a setting of 0 disables the periodic check. Valid values are a number followed by "s" for seconds, "m" for minutes, and "h" for hours; for example, `30s` for 30 seconds.

The `file` plug-in is fine if you're configuring CoreDNS as the primary DNS server for a few zones. But what if you want CoreDNS to be primary for hundreds of zones? In that case, you want the `auto` plug-in.

The auto Plug-in

The auto plug-in provides a clever way to load a large number of zones from multiple zone data files at once. This minimizes the length and complexity of the *Corefile* and provides the ability to automatically configure CoreDNS as the primary for new zones. Example 4-7 shows the syntax.

Example 4-7. Syntax of auto plug-in

```
auto [ZONES...] {
    directory DIR [REGEXP ORIGIN_TEMPLATE]
    transfer to ADDRESS...
    reload DURATION
}
```

auto tells CoreDNS to scan the directory for files matching the pattern db.*. Each file is interpreted as a zone data file whose origin is what follows db.. That origin must be within the zone or zones listed in ZONES, if specified.

Suppose that the directory */etc/coredns/zones* contains the zone data files *db.foo.example* and *db.bar.example*, which describe the zones *foo.example* and *bar.example*, respectively. The auto plug-in shown in Example 4-8 would instruct CoreDNS to read the entire directory and load the *foo.example* and *bar.example* zones from those files.

Example 4-8. An auto plug-in

```
auto example {
    directory /etc/coredns/zones
}
```

Moreover, you can create another zone (under the *example* domain, anyway) just by creating a new, appropriately named zone data file in */etc/coredns/zones*.

You can also specify a regular expression besides db.* for CoreDNS to look for in the directory, and give CoreDNS instructions on how to create the origin (and domain name of the zone) from the filename. If, for example, you named your zone data files *<domain>.zone*, you could use the auto plug-in presented in Example 4-9.

Example 4-9. Another auto plug-in

```
auto example {
    directory /etc/coredns/zones (.*)\.zone {1}
}
```

The regular expression (regex) is expected to incorporate what is essentially a Perl capture group: the parentheses around ".*" indicate the portion of the filename that contains the origin (in this case, everything before .zone); the {1} is a backreference to that portion of the regex. You can use other backreferences, of course, such as {2} for the second capture group.

Finally, you can use the file directives transfer, reload, and upstream to control which DNS servers can perform zone transfers of these zones (and receive NOTIFY messages from CoreDNS), how often the directory is scanned for modified zone data files, and which DNS servers to use to resolve external domain names.

Using the auto Plug-in with Git

Avid users of the Git distributed version-control system can easily combine the auto plug-in with a script such as git-sync (*https://github.com/kubernetes/git-sync*) to periodically pull zone data files from a Git repository into a directory. CoreDNS then scans the directory and loads new and modified zones. Using Git allows multiple administrators to jointly manage a set of version-controlled zone data files so that administrators can track changes to zone data.

git-sync is, not surprisingly, implemented as a container. Here's an example of using git-sync to periodically scan a GitHub repository for new zone data files, as demonstrated in Example 4-10.

Example 4-10. git-sync in action

```
docker run -d \
   -v /etc/coredns/zone:/tmp/git \
   registry/git-sync \
     --repo=https://github.com/myzonedata
     --branch=master
     --wait=30
```

This command uses the git-sync container to synchronize files from the *https://github.com/myzonedata* repository to */etc/coredns/zone* and to check the repository every 30 seconds for changes.

What if you have the opposite problem that auto solves—namely, that you just want to load a few resource records into CoreDNS without the overhead of a zone data file. Well then, the hosts plug-in will come in handy.

The hosts Plug-in

The `hosts` plug-in is used to configure CoreDNS to generate zone data from a host table (e.g., */etc/hosts*). The host table must be in the standard host table format:

```
<IP address> <canonical name> [aliases...]
```

The IP address can be either an IPv4 or an IPv6 address. The canonical name and any aliases must be domain names. After the host table is read, `hosts` generates the following:

- A records for each entry with an IPv4 address, mapping the canonical name and any aliases to the specified IPv4 address
- AAAA records for each entry with an IPv6 address, mapping the canonical name and any aliases to the specified IPv6 address
- A PTR record for either an IPv4 or IPv6 address, mapping the address back to the canonical name

Note that the aliases become A or AAAA records, not canonical name (CNAME) records.

Example 4-11 presents the syntax of the `hosts` plug-in.

Example 4-11. Syntax of the hosts plug-in

```
hosts [FILE [ZONES...]] {
    [INLINE]
    ttl SECONDS
    no_reverse
    reload DURATION
    fallthrough [ZONES...]
}
```

`FILE` specifies the name of the hosts file to read and parse; by default, CoreDNS reads */etc/hosts*. If `FILE` is a relative pathname, it's interpreted relative to the directory specified in the `ROOT` directive.

`ZONES` is an optional list of one or more zones that are loaded from the host table. If `ZONES` isn't specified, CoreDNS uses the zones from the enclosing server block. Domain names will be loaded only into the zones of which they are a part. In other words, if you load the host table shown in Example 4-12 as both *foo.example* and *bar.example*, you'll end up with *host1.foo.example* in the *foo.example* zone and *host2.bar.example* in *bar.example*.

Example 4-12. Example host table

```
10.0.0.1 host1.foo.example
10.0.1.1 host2.bar.example
```

Zones whose data is read using the hosts plug-in aren't really complete zones; they don't have SOA records, for example, so they can't be transferred to another DNS server. Consequently, hosts isn't usually used for management of an entire zone; rather, you would use it for loading discrete domain names. For example, some people load a host table that includes domain names used in serving ads and that maps those domain names to the IP address 0.0.0.0.

[INLINE] allows you to specify one or more lines in host table format directly in the directive, as shown in Example 4-13.

Example 4-13. Inline host table entries

```
foo.example {
    hosts {
        10.0.0.1 host1.foo.example
        10.0.1.1 host2.foo.example
    }
}
```

TTL sets the time-to-live (TTL) value for records synthesized from host table entries; by default, the TTL is set to 3600 seconds, or 1 hour. The value must be specified as an integer (in other words, don't specify units such as "s" for seconds).

no_reverse inhibits the creation of PTR records from host table entries.

By default, CoreDNS reloads the host table every 5 seconds. reload allows you to change this interval by specifying a scaled value (i.e., a number followed by a unit of time) with the following units:

- ns for nanoseconds
- us or µs for microseconds
- ms for milliseconds
- s for seconds
- m for minutes
- h for hours

I'm not sure you really need the ability to specify a reload interval of 500,000,000 nanoseconds (with 500000000 ns), but with CoreDNS, you can!

Finally, fallthrough controls whether queries for the zones handled by the hosts plug-in fall through to another plug-in if no answer is found. For example, you might want queries for *foo.example* to fall through from the hosts plug-in to a file plug-in if the answer wasn't found in the host table. By default, specifying `fallthrough` instructs CoreDNS to fall through for any queries handled by the `hosts` plug-in. To fall through only for a subset of those queries, you can specify a list of zones as an argument.

Next, we look at a way to load zone data from Amazon's Route 53 service.

The route53 plug-in

Many organizations use the Amazon Route 53 service to provide authoritative DNS services from the Amazon Web Services (AWS) cloud. CoreDNS provides a plug-in, `route53`, that enables it to synchronize zone data from Route 53, much like a secondary DNS server would transfer zone data from a master DNS server. CoreDNS can then respond authoritatively to queries for domain names in the synchronized zone.

Example 4-14. Syntax of the route53 plug-in

```
route53 [ZONE:HOSTED_ZONE_ID...] {
    [aws_access_key AWS_ACCESS_KEY_ID AWS_SECRET_ACCESS_KEY]
    upstream
    credentials PROFILE [FILENAME]
    fallthrough [ZONES...]
}
```

To synchronize the zone, CoreDNS must provide the domain name of the zone and a special "Hosted Zone ID" used within AWS as well as credentials that authenticate CoreDNS to Route 53.[1] To get the zone ID, log in to the AWS Dashboard, go to the Route 53 service, and then click "Hosted zones." This should bring up a table of zones that includes each zone's Hosted Zone ID.

The `route53` plug-in requires that you specify the domain name of the zone and the Hosted Zone ID in a particular (and particularly inflexible) format: the domain name of the zone, terminated with a dot, followed by a colon, then the Hosted Zone ID. Example 4-15 demonstrates this format.

Example 4-15. The route53 plug-in

```
route53 foo.example.:Z3CDX6AOCUSMX3 {
    fallthrough
}
```

---

1 The Hosted Zone ID uniquely identifies the zone to AWS. The domain name of the zone alone isn't always enough, because AWS might have Public Hosted Zones and Private Hosted Zones with the same domain name.

You can specify multiple zones if you want CoreDNS to synchronize all of them from Route 53.

By default, CoreDNS determines the AWS credentials to use from environment variables or an AWS credentials file. You can override this behavior by specifying the credentials directly within the route53 plug-in, as illustrated in Example 4-16.

Example 4-16. route53 plug-in with explicit credentials

```
route53 foo.example.:Z3CDX6AOCUSMX3 {
    aws_access_key AKIAIMSX7F33X4MOVBZA SnA4XxFPx/BDEMbty3EKVze7Xi3DkQ5a8akRO9j9
}
```

You can also specify an AWS credentials file other than the default using the credentials subdirective shown in Example 4-17.

Example 4-17. route53 plug-in with credentials file

```
route53 foo.example.:Z3CDX6AOCUSMX3 {
    credentials default .awscredentials
}
```

default, in this case, specifies a particular profile in the credentials file.

Like hosts, the route53 plug-in supports fallthrough to other plug-ins, for all or a specified set of zones synchronized from Route 53. And, like file, route53 supports specification of an upstream DNS server to resolve references to external domain names in the Route 53 zone data.

That's the last of the plug-ins for managing zone data in CoreDNS. Hopefully, among the four options (five if you count using the auto plug-in with Git), you'll find one that meets your needs.

Although CoreDNS is a flexible and capable primary DNS server, its strength, of course, is supporting DNS-based service discovery. We cover that in Chapter 5.

Service Discovery

Introduction to Service Discovery

As described in Chapter 1, CoreDNS is designed to be flexible for new use cases that are not part of the traditional DNS landscape. Many of these use cases come out of the current industry-wide movement from monolithic application architectures to microservice-based architectures.

In microservice architectures, applications are broken into small, independent functional components. Each of these components is the master of its own set of functionality and associated data. For example, a simple online retail application might be broken down into the following independent microservices:

- User Profile
- Product Catalog
- Shopping Cart
- Checkout
- Shipping Cost
- Payment

Microservices

There are many ways to break up any given application into microservices. Often complex applications can be broken into dozens or even hundreds of microservices. For more on this, see Sam Newman's *Monolith to Microservices* (O'Reilly).

For the application to complete complex workflows and logic, varying microservices must communicate with one another. For example, for the Checkout service to calculate the final price, it needs to gather the list of items from the Shopping Cart, the item prices from the Product Catalog, and the shipping fees from the Shipping Cost service. In a microservice architecture, each of these services provides an application programming interface (API) (as a network service) from which the data can be collected. How does the Checkout service know what IP address and port to use to connect to each of these APIs? The answer is using a service discovery function in a microservice architecture, which we cover throughout this chapter.

DNS Service Discovery

RFC 6763 defines a mechanism called DNS Service Discovery or DNS-SD. The service discovery discussed here does not refer to the specific implementation described in that RFC, but to the more general class of problem. The focus in this section is on application components discovering other application components, not on discovery of general network services for end users. CoreDNS does not offer any specialized support for DNS-SD at this time.

Solving the Service Discovery Problem

Let's look at a few ways to accomplish service discovery in this example. The first is to simply pass the IP address and port into the Checkout service as a command-line argument when it starts up. This works well if your service endpoints never change, but if you need to move a service to a different IP address for maintenance, due to a failure, or for any other reason, you might need to reconfigure and restart all dependent services.

This is the sort of problem that host names were originally designed to solve: instead of passing IP addresses, we can pass in names. Those names can be stored in each client's */etc/hosts* files, and we can distribute those files (or the names they should contain) to every client. In a containerized environment using Docker, this was an early approach taken. The Docker daemon provided a now-deprecated `-link` command-line option. This option modifies the containers' *hosts* files to point the names at the appropriate IP addresses. Note the "now-deprecated" description of that option. This technique proved to be ineffective, because it is error prone and quickly creates a lot of management overhead. It also worked only for containers on the same host and had some inherent race conditions that caused failures.

To avoid these problems with distributing or modifying */etc/hosts* files, the next logical step is to move to centralized distribution of names and IPs; that is, to use domain names stored in DNS. Using DNS provides a level of indirection as with *hosts* files, but allows the mapping to change. This lets us move a service without having to explicitly reconfigure every client of that service.

With a DNS server rather than *hosts* files, we also get the richer set of record types that DNS supports, rather than just the host/IP mappings from */etc/hosts*. The names can correspond to SRV records, for example, instead of just A records. An SRV record contains a port as well as another DNS name, which can be resolved to an IP address. Using an SRV record means we do not need to follow ordinary port conventions for services, allowing us to host, for example, multiple HTTP-based microservice APIs on the same IP address. In simple containerized environments, only the host's IP address is reachable on the network, and containers are reached by forwarding ports from the host IP address to the host-local container IP addresses. Without the ability to discover port numbers in addition to IP addresses, we would be limited to running only a single container providing an HTTP service, or we would need to fall back to the difficult-to-manage static service/port mappings.

So, does this solve the service discovery problem for microservices? Can we simply set up, say, a BIND server and call it a day? Not quite. The microservice environment is a bit different from a traditional environment. In a traditional environment, the expectation is that A records (and SRV records that refer to them) reference relatively static data corresponding to host names. That is, the design of traditional DNS servers is focused on serving data at global scale, with time-to-live (TTL) settings on the order of minutes or hours. The workflows for managing the data are often manual, or they at least rely on files that must be modified and reloaded, and perhaps then propagated to secondary DNS servers.

In microservice environments, it's possible that the IP addresses for a given service are changing much more rapidly than in traditional environments. Microservices can be scaled up and down by starting and stopping Linux containers. This is generally much faster than spinning up new virtual machines (VMs)—on the order of a second or two, versus several minutes. This means that the data served by the service discovery function can become stale very quickly. This doesn't lend itself to manual configuration of zone files.

Specialized *service registration and discovery* products such as HashiCorp's Consul have arisen to fill this niche. These products provide an API-based mechanism to register a service and then make the service location available via an API and DNS. A typical pattern is for services to self-register with the service registration and discovery agent. When a new instance of a service comes up, it makes an API call to the registry and identifies itself and its location. Alternatively, the controller or orchestrator that is launching the process can make the API call to register it. Either method is much faster than requiring an administrator to modify a zone file and reloading named.

Even with this dynamic, API-based registration, clients do not find out about service location changes. They must still rely on a TTL and requery the service discovery to find out whether a service has moved or whether a new instance is available. To minimize this, service discovery solutions often provide a method to push data to clients, rather than using a traditional DNS-style TTL. This reduces the failed requests due to a microservice instance scaling down, and it maximizes the spread of traffic among newly spun up microservice instances.

DNS does not provide any push-based functionality today. So purpose-built service discovery products such as Consul implement alternate protocols to provide this feature. To provide a similar level of functionality, CoreDNS relies on gRPC Remote Procedure Call (gRPC),[1] which is an open source, HTTP/2-based remote procedure call interface originally created at Google. gRPC implements many different remote call semantics, including ordinary synchronous request/reply, asynchronous request/reply, and a push mechanism. It's this last one that some versions of CoreDNS used to implement an experimental push-based service discovery. Current versions of CoreDNS do not provide this feature, but it might be added back in the future, based on demand.

DNS-over-gRPC

CoreDNS defines a gRPC service for querying names. The protocol itself simply embeds a DNS packet inside of a Protocol Buffer (Protobuf) message. This is not a standard, and as far as the CoreDNS developers know, is not used anywhere but within CoreDNS itself. It does provide the basis for the push-based, experimental service discovery described here, but it should be noted that gRPC is a much less efficient protocol than standard DNS. Based on internal analysis done at Infoblox, a single query that is one packet sent and one received with standard User Datagram Protocol (UDP) can result in *eight* packets exchanged when using gRPC.

Now that we understand the need for a central discovery service, we can take a look at how CoreDNS can help by combining it with a key–value database.

Service Discovery with CoreDNS and etcd

etcd is a distributed key–value data store developed by CoreOS[2] (no relation to CoreDNS, despite the name) to help coordinate upgrades of fleets of Linux machines. It

---

1 In the tradition of the Free Software Foundation's GNU's Not Unix! (GNU), gRPC is a recursive acronym that stands for "gRPC Remote Procedure Call."

2 CoreOS was bought by Red Hat, which has since been bought by IBM.

---

implements specialized algorithms for leader election and to coordinate distributed writes that can be read consistently from any instance. This makes etcd very resilient to individual failures. As long as the running instances can achieve *quorum*—that is, as long as more than half of the instances are up and able to communicate with one another—etcd will keep running and accepting reads and writes. For example, if you have deployed three instances of etcd as a cluster, you can lose any one of them and the system will continue to function.

The distributed, resilient design of etcd makes it a good fit in containerized microservice environments, which are also highly distributed. In these environments, components are expected to fail, and so all aspects of the applications and their dependencies must be resilient and continue to operate in as many failure modes as possible.

The etcd Plug-in

CoreDNS integration with etcd is through the `etcd` plug-in. This plug-in reads data from etcd directly using the `etcdv3` API,[3] for the expressed purpose of service discovery. In fact, it is designed to be compatible with an older service discovery application called SkyDNS, of which Miek Gieben, the lead developer for CoreDNS, was also an author. In part, CoreDNS was designed to become the "110%" replacement for SkyDNS—"a better SkyDNS than SkyDNS," he likes to say. Because of this history, the `etcd` plug-in does not provide a general-purpose DNS server backed by etcd; it is really focused on the service discovery use case and thus has some limitations.

When using CoreDNS and etcd for service registry and discovery, all of the persistent state (data) is stored in etcd. CoreDNS connects to etcd and reads data as needed based on queries and the contents of its cache (if enabled). It is important to isolate the state into a redundant data store to avoid losing information when a component fails. Running as a stateless service also makes it much simpler to scale CoreDNS; we can run many instances behind a load balancer to handle our traffic load.

So what does the data look like in etcd? Recall that etcd is a key–value store. This means that you can provide a key, and it will return a value. With SkyDNS—and therefore with this plug-in—each service is represented by a particular key corresponding to the service name. Before CoreDNS can serve records from etcd, we need to populate etcd with these records.

---

3 CoreDNS versions prior to 1.2.0 use the older `etcdv2` API, but that is not supported in versions after CoreDNS 1.2.0.

SkyDNS Message format

For the `etcd` plug-in, services are stored in etcd using a format that was developed for SkyDNS. The keys used are derived from the service names, and the values contain the *SkyDNS Message*.[4] The SkyDNS Message is a JSON-encoded object, as shown in Example 5-1.

Example 5-1. Sample SkyDNS Message

```
{
 "host": "192.0.2.10",
 "port": 20020,
 "priority": 10,
 "weight": 20
}
```

This just shows a few fields that are used when registering services on different ports. The `host` field is used to hold the IP address of our service, and the `port`, `priority`, and `weight` fields are used when generating SRV records for the service. Notice that the fields other than `host` are not in quotes. This is because they are integers and so JSON must encode them that way; otherwise, they will not be retrieved properly by CoreDNS. There are a number of additional fields that we can use to make additional record types available. The most useful of these is probably `ttl`, which allows you to specify the TTL for the various records this service registration entry generates. You can see all the details on the SkyDNS GitHub.

To answer queries for this service via the `etcd` plug-in, we need to store this object in etcd under a specific key. The format of the key is structured like a Unix directory path, going in the reverse order of the domain name. The root of the path is, by default `/skydns`, although this is configurable. If we want to make our example service available as the name *users.services.example.com*, we populate etcd with the JSON object above, at the key `/skydns/com/example/services/users`. An example of how to do this is shown in Example 5-3, but first we need to get etcd up and running.

Running etcd

For purposes of trying out the examples, you can download and run etcd. It is available for many different platforms on the etcd release page at *https://github.com/etcd-io/etcd/releases*. Because it is a statically linked executable, it should run in your environment without any dependencies. Just running it as shown in Example 5-2, without any arguments, is fine for these exercises.

---

4 See the SkyDNS GitHub (*https://oreil.ly/W1iTk*) for full details.

Example 5-2. Running etcd

```
$ ./etcd
2019-01-16 05:28:10.138321 I | etcdmain: etcd Version: 3.3.11
2019-01-16 05:28:10.138414 I | etcdmain: Git SHA: 2cf9e51d2
2019-01-16 05:28:10.138432 I | etcdmain: Go Version: go1.10.7
2019-01-16 05:28:10.138444 I | etcdmain: Go OS/Arch: linux/amd64
...
```

After this is up and running, you can populate it with some messages using the etcdctl command, which is part of the release package. By default, etcdctl uses the ectdv2 API, so we must specify an environment variable to direct it to use the etcdv3 API. To store the JSON message shown in Example 5-1, you use the etcdctl put command. Example 5-3 shows storing and retrieving this entry with etdctl.

Example 5-3. Populating a SkyDNS Message

```
$ ETCDCTL_API=3 ./etcdctl put /skydns/com/example/services/users \
    '{"host": "192.0.2.10","port ": 20020,"priority": 10,"weight": 20}'
OK
$ ETCDCTL_API=3 ./etcdctl get /skydns/com/example/services/users
/skydns/com/example/services/users
{"host": "192.0.2.10","port": 20020,"priority": 10,"weight": 20}
```

Now that there is an entry in etcd, we can take a look at how to configure CoreDNS to serve up that entry via DNS.

Configuration syntax

In its simplest form, you can use the plug-in simply by including the etcd directive. The *Corefile* in Example 5-4 will serve example.com on port 5300, with the etcd plug-in. The plug-in will connect via gRPC (HTTP) to the local etcd instance or proxy, on the default etcd port; that is, to the URL http://localhost:2379.

Example 5-4. Corefile: simplest etcd configuration

```
example.com:5300 {
 etcd
}
```

You can also provide a list of zones after the etcd directive, to restrict the list to a specific set of zones. Without those, it will use the zones from the server stanza (example.com in this case).

Example 5-5 illustrates this. The etcd plug-in will be used to serve services.example.com, and all other queries will be served by the forward plug-in, which is covered in "Forward" on page 42.

Example 5-5. Corefile: etcd plug-in with restricted zones

```
example.com:5300 {
  log
  etcd services.example.com
  forward example.com /etc/resolv.conf
}
```

Run CoreDNS with that *Corefile* using `coredns -conf Corefile-etcd-1`. We can then test this by querying for our service by using `dig` in another terminal window, as demonstrated in Example 5-6.

Example 5-6. An etcd plug-in query

```
$ dig -p 5300 users.services.example.com @localhost

; <<>> DiG 9.10.3-P4-Debian <<>> -p 5300 users.services.example.com @localhost
;; global options: +cmd
;; Got answer:
;; ->>HEADER<<- opcode: QUERY, status: NOERROR, id: 36464
;; flags: qr aa rd; QUERY: 1, ANSWER: 1, AUTHORITY: 0, ADDITIONAL: 1
;; WARNING: recursion requested but not available

;; OPT PSEUDOSECTION:
; EDNS: version: 0, flags:; udp: 4096
;; QUESTION SECTION:
;users.services.example.com.     IN    A

;; ANSWER SECTION:
users.services.example.com. 300 IN    A        192.0.2.10

;; Query time: 2 msec
;; SERVER: ::1#5300(::1)
;; WHEN: Wed Jan 16 06:48:07 UTC 2019
;; MSG SIZE  rcvd: 97
```

This returns our expected A record with the IP we registered in etcd. But this registration also returns other types of records, in particular an SRV record that will include the port, as shown in Example 5-7.

Example 5-7. An SRV query with etcd plug-in

```
$ dig -p 5300 -t SRV users.services.example.com @localhost

; <<>> DiG 9.10.3-P4-Debian <<>> -p 5300 -t SRV users.services.example.com @localhost
;; global options: +cmd
;; Got answer:
;; ->>HEADER<<- opcode: QUERY, status: NOERROR, id: 57074
;; flags: qr aa rd; QUERY: 1, ANSWER: 1, AUTHORITY: 0, ADDITIONAL: 2
```

```
;; WARNING: recursion requested but not available

;; OPT PSEUDOSECTION:
; EDNS: version: 0, flags:; udp: 4096
;; QUESTION SECTION:
;users.services.example.com.      IN    SRV

;; ANSWER SECTION:
users.services.example.com. 300 IN    SRV     10 100 20020 users.services.example.com.

;; ADDITIONAL SECTION:
users.services.example.com. 300 IN    A       192.0.2.10

;; Query time: 4 msec
;; SERVER: ::1#5300(::1)
;; WHEN: Wed Jan 16 06:57:32 UTC 2019
;; MSG SIZE  rcvd: 169
```

Back in your CoreDNS terminal, you should see output similar to that shown in Example 5-8, with log entries for each of the queries we attempted.

Example 5-8. Running CoreDNS with etcd

```
$ ./coredns -conf Corefile-etcd
example.com.:5300
2019-01-16T06:59:17.261Z [INFO] CoreDNS-1.3.1
2019-01-16T06:59:17.261Z [INFO] linux/amd64, go1.11.4, 6b56a9c
CoreDNS-1.3.1
linux/amd64, go1.11.4, 6b56a9c
2019-01-16T06:59:24.341Z [INFO] [::1]:57999 - 58777 "A IN users.services.example...
2019-01-16T06:59:26.516Z [INFO] [::1]:33437 - 43373 "SRV IN users.services.example...
```

That covers the basic use of the etcd plug-in. Next, let's look at the complete syntax.

Complete syntax

A number of additional options are available for this plug-in:

```
etcd [ZONES...] {
    stubzones
    fallthrough [ZONES...]
    path PATH
    endpoint ENDPOINT...
    credentials USERNAME PASSWORD
    upstream [ADDRESS...]
    tls CERT KEY CACERT
}
```

Following is a description of each of the optional configuration keys:

`stubzones`
> This enables the SkyDNS-like stub domain feature. This allows the plug-in to forward queries for a set of domains to different nameservers. The domains and nameservers are stored in etcd. This is provided only for backward compatibility when migrating from SkyDNS and, in fact, is only valid in versions of CoreDNS before 1.4.0. The recommended approach to achieve the same result in current versions of CoreDNS is to use `forward`, as discussed in "Forward" on page 42, along with the `fallthrough` option.

`fallthrough`
> This allows queries for the listed zones to be passed down the plug-in chain to later plug-ins, as described in "fallthrough" on page 50.

`path`
> Allows you to overide the default `/skydns` path with another base path.

`endpoint`
> This is used to specify a list of etcd API endpoints to use. For example, `endpoint https://192.0.2.2:2379 https://192.0.2.3:2379 https://192.0.2.4:2379` would enable any of those three endpoints to be used, in order to provide highly available access to etcd.

`credentials`
> This is used to specify the username and password for the etcd server. It is available starting in CoreDNS 1.4.0.

`upstream`
> This is used for looking up the A record corresponding to canonical name (CNAME) records, but is obsolete in CoreDNS 1.3.0 and later.

`tls`
> This is used to configure the Transport Layer Security (TLS) client parameters for connecting to etcd, as described in "tls" on page 50.

Next, we take a look at some additional service discovery options.

Other Service Discovery Options

Of course, etcd is just one possible data store for service registration. For another dynamic option, you can use a relational database. CoreDNS does not ship with a built-in plug-in for access data from a SQL database, but there is an external plug-in, `pdsql`, that makes this possible. (We show you how to build CoreDNS with an external plug-in in "Modifying plugin.cfg" on page 161.) A somewhat less dynamic option would be to use the `hosts` plug-in, which can read a file in the standard */etc/hosts* format, as descibed in "The hosts Plug-in" on page 60. CoreDNS will check the file for changes every 5 seconds, so you can change your DNS records with changes to a simple file.

That covers the basic service discovery options using CoreDNS, except for the case of using CoreDNS with container orchestration, which we discuss next.

Service Discovery and Container Orchestration

In "Solving the Service Discovery Problem" on page 66, we mentioned that services need to be registered with the service discovery solution. For example, when using CoreDNS and etcd, something needs to write the entry in etcd. In containerized environments (as opposed to environments using VMs), this registration would now be handled more often by a container orchestrator such as Kubernetes.

 As of Kubernetes 1.13, CoreDNS is the default service discovery solution for Kubernetes.

Even with the orchestrator populating the registry in the container use case, there are still many environments and applications that require service discovery as described here. If an application requires spinning up VMs rather than containers, it is necessary to fall back on using these techniques. One of the advantages of CoreDNS over other service discovery options is that it can handle both of these scenarios, and can even support both in the same server instance.

This chapter covered the basics of service discovery, and how to perform service discovery in dynamic environments using CoreDNS and etcd. Chapter 6 goes in depth on the specific use case of how CoreDNS is used in Kubernetes clusters. This is an important topic to which we have devoted the entire chapter.

Kubernetes

Kubernetes has become the dominant solution for managing container-based services. As a sibling Cloud Native Computing Foundation (CNCF) project, the CoreDNS community has also been closely involved in the Kubernetes community. After adding initial support for zone data files and for replacing SkyDNS's functionality, the CoreDNS community began working on integrating with Kubernetes.

We chose to integrate with Kubernetes prior to the other container orchestration systems[1] for two primary reasons. One was that the existing Kubernetes DNS service, *kube-dns,* was based on SkyDNS, and we saw an opportunity to improve its functioning. Additionally, the openness of the Kubernetes API made integrating with it much easier than with other container orchestration solutions.

In this chapter, we first discuss the basics of Kubernetes. This includes some of its internal structure and the principles behind its design and the different types of network services defined by Kubernetes. Next, the section on the DNS specification for Kubernetes explains how those different types of services are represented in the DNS records. Finally we discuss how CoreDNS itself is configured to run and scale within a Kubernetes cluster, and some special features and optimizations that CoreDNS provides beyond the standard Kubernetes functionality.

Basic Concepts

To understand how DNS fits into Kubernetes and how CoreDNS integrates with it, you must have a clear understanding of some of the basic concepts in Kubernetes. We go over the essentials here, but there are a number of excellent books on the subject,

---

1 The other systems on our roadmap were *Mesos/Marathon* and *Docker Swarm.*

such as *Kubernetes: Up and Running: Dive into the Future of Infrastructure* (O'Reilly) by Kelsey Hightower, Brendan Burns, and Joe Beda.

Kubernetes is a set of software components for managing workloads across a distributed set of machines, called a *cluster*. Machines that are part of the cluster are called *nodes*. Nodes are often partitioned into *master* and *worker* nodes, though this is not strictly necessary. The master nodes run the core control-plane components, whereas the worker nodes run user workloads, along with a minimal set of control-plane components needed to operate as part of the cluster.

When a workload is deployed on a Kubernetes cluster, it is deployed as a set of *pods*. A pod is a set of closely related containers, along with some shared resources such as the networking stack. That is, all containers running in a pod share the same Linux network namespace. From the containers' points of view, they are all running on the same networked host. A pod is the unit of scale in Kubernetes. If you want to scale an application up, you add additional pods serving that application.

The heart of the control plane is the *API server*, through which all other components coordinate. The Kubernetes API is an HTTP-based, resource-oriented API that follows common representational state transfer (REST) conventions. Most of the operations are simply creating, reading, updating, or deleting (CRUD) resources. The API server is backed by the etcd distributed key–value store, which is where these various resources are stored. Users interact with the API via the `kubectl` client program, or directly using HTTP.

The Kubernetes API is a *declarative* API. This means that the client uses the API to declare the desired state of the cluster, and it is up to Kubernetes to render *and maintain* that state. This is as opposed to a more conventional *imperative* API, which executes a one-time operation. To illustrate the difference, consider a hypothetical API to run a process. To use an imperative API, the client would send a command to run, and the server would execute the command and return. With a declarative API, the client would send the API a declaration that there should always be a process running based on the command. It is the responsibility of the system implementing that declarative API to launch the process and then monitor and ensure that the process is always running. If the process crashes, the imperative API implementation knows nothing about it—it has already exited and does not track the state of the process. The declarative API implementation must monitor the process, notice that it has failed, and restart it. So long as the resource declaring the intent for this process to run exists, the system will ensure that the process is there. In some literature, you might also see declarative APIs referred to as *intent-based* APIs.

In Kubernetes, the components that ensure the intended state are called *controllers*. Typically, a controller manages a set of related resources by executing a *reconciliation loop*. This is an infinite loop that does the following:

1. Reads the intended resource state from the API server. Most often this is defined in the Spec field of the resource.
2. Observes the current state of the resource, either by reading the Status field of the resource, or by directly observing the cluster, or some combination of the two.
3. Attempts to reconcile any difference between the desired and observed states by taking appropriate action. As it modifies the state, it will store the progress in the Status field so that users (or other controllers) have visibility into the process.

From this description, it is clear that the controller must be continually monitoring a given resource in order to know whether there has been a change to the desired state. One way to do this would be to have the controller poll the API server with each iteration through the reconciliation loop. This is simple but has some drawbacks. When the user changes the desired state, the controller will not react until the next poll. To avoid a sluggish response to changes, a very short interval between polls is necessary. However, frequent polling puts a large load on the API server, which will cause its own delays, waste resources, and limit the scalability of the overall solution.

The API server solves this problem with a *watch* feature that is not commonly seen in other RESTful APIs. When a client queries for a particular resource, it can create a persistent connection and ask the server to push any updates to the resources through that connection. This behavior avoids polling and is critical to the efficient operation of a Kubernetes cluster. Controllers use this feature to keep track of the intended state of their resources, without needing to repeatedly poll the API server.

That covers the API server where users interact and resources are stored, and the controllers that monitor changes in resources and then take some action. But how is that action taken? Controllers do not run on every node: they run only on control plane nodes. To take some action—for example, create a pod—on a node, we need another piece of software installed on that node. This is the last critical infrastructure component, the *kubelet*. The kubelet is an agent that runs on every node, and is responsible for launching, monitoring, and destroying pods and managing other node-level resources. It also reports the node capabilities and state to the API server, so that the scheduler can choose the node for a new pod.

Deploying all of these pods across different machines is great, but if you want them to be able find and talk to one another, you will need some networking between pods. This is the topic of the next section.

Kubernetes Networking

The previous section covered the basic components and functions of the primary Kubernetes control plane. Layered on top of those functions are the networking services, including DNS and load balancing. Although these functions are technically "add-on" (optional) features, the majority of clusters deploy them. In this section, we describe how Kubernetes provides load balancing for services running in the cluster, and the expectations for cluster DNS. These two topics are closely linked.

Suppose that you have a service running in a pod that you would like to make available to the other clients running in the cluster. Every pod gets an IP address. In every Kubernetes cluster, all pods have to be able to reach any other pod.[2] So, we could simply let every client know our pod IP, and they would be able to reach us.

Of course, that's not a very effective method. Pods can come and go, especially pods that are managed by a *Deployment*. In Deployments, pods are considered to be identical replicas that can be scaled up and down or replaced due to crashing or application upgrades. Each time a pod is destroyed and recreated, a new IP address is allocated. We cannot expect IP addresses to be stable in this environment. Additionally, if there are multiple pods providing the service, we would need to communicate all of those addresses as they come and go.

Kubernetes solves this problem with a *Service* resource. This resource combines a load-balancing configuration, a way to select pods that provide the Service, and a name. For advertising a Service to other clients in the cluster, there are two types of Services that are relevant: *cluster IP* Services and *headless* Services.

Cluster IP Services

Cluster IP Services solve exactly the problem we described earlier: they create a stable, cluster-wide virtual IP (VIP) address for a Service, and associate it with a name. All pods providing a Service are given specific labels, and the Service is provided with a selector for those labels. The selector is used to select pods and group them into *Endpoints* resources, which contain all of the addresses and ports of those resources. Example 6-1 shows a cluster IP Service.

Example 6-1. Cluster IP Service

```
apiVersion: v1
kind: Service
metadata:
  name: hello-world
  namespace: default
spec:
  selector:
    app: hello-world
  type: ClusterIP
```

---

2 In some Kubernetes networking implementations, you can control communication between pods by using a *network policy* feature.

```
clusterIP: 10.0.0.100
ports:
 - name: http
   port: 80
   protocol: TCP
```

In this example, pods that have the label `app` with value `hello-world` will be selected as part of the service, and their addresses will be stored in an `Endpoints` object with the same name as the service. To actually load balance traffic across those pods, there is another component of the control plane needed. This is a binary that runs on each node, called a *kube-proxy*. It manipulates the netfilter tables of the node using the standard Linux `iptables`, so that traffic bound for the VIP is randomly redirected to one of the endpoint addresses.

Headless Services

The headless service looks exactly like a cluster IP service, except that the `clusterIP` field is set to `None`, as shown in Example 6-2. In this case, there is no VIP, and kube-proxy ignores the service. Instead, any load balancing is done in the client itself, using DNS to find all of the IP addresses for the service. The gRPC Remote Procedure Call (gRPC) authors, for example, recommend client-side load balancing when using that protocol. The downside to this is that the client is responsible for actively reresolving the queries to identify any changes to the set of endpoints.

Example 6-2. Headless service

```
apiVersion: v1
kind: Service
metadata:
  name: headless
  namespace: default
spec:
  selector:
    app: headless
  type: ClusterIP
  clusterIP: None
  ports:
   - name: http
     port: 80
     protocol: TCP
```

Headless services are also useful for applications that must discover a fixed set of peers. For example, when running an etcd cluster, each instance needs to discover the other etcd instances in the cluster. If one of those instances changes names, etcd may encounter problems. Kubernetes solves the issue of ensuring that a set of workloads comes up with a consistent name using a *StatefulSet*. This is a workload management resource similar to the ReplicaSet seen when using a Deployment. The difference is that it does not treat each pod that it launches as an identical replica. Instead, each pod is given an ordinal number (0, 1, 2, etc.) and is named, created, and scaled in this order, and persistent volumes are reconnected with the correct pod when a pod is destroyed and recreated. When used in combination with a headless service, a stateful set can provide a stable network identity (name) for each pod, as you will see in the next section.

In fact, the next section covers how all of these different types of services are represented in the DNS service of Kubernetes through discussion of the standard Kubernetes DNS specification.

Kubernetes DNS Specification

DNS is considered an "add-on" in Kubernetes, and the cluster will function without it. However, very few clusters run without DNS, and the DNS specification for Kubernetes is considered part of the standard conformance suite. A distribution cannot declare that it is a conforming Kubernetes distribution without providing a DNS service that follows the specification (*https://oreil.ly/X8Ou-*).[3] The specification defines the DNS names that can be used to locate services running in the cluster.

This specification is an opinionated, prescribed DNS schema. That is, it defines a specific set of names that must exist based on the contents of the API server. Kubernetes Service resources are the primary way in which users can specify their intent for how services are discovered.

All records in the specification fall under a single domain, the *cluster domain*. Often, you will see the cluster domain set to `cluster.local`, which is what you will usually see in examples that you find online. In some managed solutions such as Google Kubernetes Engine (GKE), you cannot change this domain, but the vanilla open source Kubernetes allows you to choose any domain.

The specification requires that for each cluster IP, there is an A record containing the cluster IP, with a name derived from the service name and namespace: `service.namespace.svc.cluster-domain`. For example, if the Service defined in Example 6-1 were deployed in a cluster with the cluster domain `cluster.exam ple.com`, `dig` would behave as shown in Example 6-3.

---

3 The only current exception to this is that Windows-based workloads cannot use the "short-name" queries, because Windows does not provide the same search path behavior as Linux.

Example 6-3. Cluster IP Service records

```
dnstools# dig hello-world.default.svc.cluster.example.com

; <<>> DiG 9.11.3 <<>> hello-world.default.svc.cluster.example.com
;; global options: +cmd
;; Got answer:
;; ->>HEADER<<- opcode: QUERY, status: NOERROR, id: 53657
;; flags: qr aa rd; QUERY: 1, ANSWER: 1, AUTHORITY: 0, ADDITIONAL: 1
;; WARNING: recursion requested but not available

;; OPT PSEUDOSECTION:
; EDNS: version: 0, flags:; udp: 4096
; COOKIE: 6cf943d261c57648 (echoed)
;; QUESTION SECTION:
;hello-world.default.svc.cluster.example.com. IN        A

;; ANSWER SECTION:
hello-world.default.svc.cluster.example.com. 5 IN A 10.0.0.100

;; Query time: 1 msec
;; SERVER: 10.7.245.28#53(10.7.245.28)
;; WHEN: Sat Mar 02 01:36:40 UTC 2019
;; MSG SIZE  rcvd: 143
```

The dnstools Image

Many examples in this chapter are run from a pod running the
infoblox/dnstools container image. This is a publicly available
image on Docker Hub that contains DNS-specific utilities such as
host, dig, and dnsperf, as well as general networking tools including curl and tcpdump. To run a dnstools pod, use the following:

```
$ kubectl run --restart=Never -it --image \
infoblox/dnstools dnstools
dnstools#
```

There will also be a corresponding PTR record for the cluster IP.

For headless services, there are A records for every endpoint IP address for the service, at the same names described for cluster IP services. This allows you to use
client-side load balancing instead of the netfilter-based load balancing of a cluster IP.
This means that the same name will return multiple addresses, as shown
in Example 6-4.

Example 6-4. Headless service A records

```
dnstools# dig -t a headless.default.svc.cluster.local.
; <<>> DiG 9.11.3 <<>> -t a headless.default.svc.cluster.local.
;; global options: +cmd
;; Got answer:
;; WARNING: .local is reserved for Multicast DNS
;; You are currently testing what happens when an mDNS query is leaked to DNS
;; ->>HEADER<<- opcode: QUERY, status: NOERROR, id: 44753
;; flags: qr aa rd; QUERY: 1, ANSWER: 4, AUTHORITY: 0, ADDITIONAL: 1
;; WARNING: recursion requested but not available
;; OPT PSEUDOSECTION:
; EDNS: version: 0, flags:; udp: 4096
; COOKIE: b42f2304777ada80 (echoed)
;; QUESTION SECTION:
;headless.default.svc.cluster.local. IN A
;; ANSWER SECTION:
headless.default.svc.cluster.local. 5 IN A      10.5.88.4
headless.default.svc.cluster.local. 5 IN A      10.5.88.6
headless.default.svc.cluster.local. 5 IN A      10.5.88.7
headless.default.svc.cluster.local. 5 IN A      10.5.88.5
;; Query time: 1 msec
;; SERVER: 10.7.240.9#53(10.7.240.9)
;; WHEN: Mon Mar 18 03:25:02 UTC 2019
;; MSG SIZE  rcvd: 275
```

In addition to the A records, there are SRV records for each endpoint address and named-port combination. An SRV record includes not only the IP address, but also the port, and you query it by port name and protocol. In Example 6-5, you can see how to query an SRV record using dig. Normally, underscores are not allowed in DNS names. However, RFC 2782, which defines the SRV record, uses the underscore to denote that these labels are not ordinary parts of the name; rather, they are reserved for the port name and protocol, specifically. In this case, we are querying to find an HTTP service running over TCP.

Example 6-5. Headless service SRV records

```
dnstools# dig -t srv _http._tcp.headless.default.svc.cluster.local.


; <<>> DiG 9.11.3 <<>> -t srv _http._tcp.headless.default.svc.cluster.local.
;; global options: +cmd
;; Got answer:
;; WARNING: .local is reserved for Multicast DNS
;; You are currently testing what happens when an mDNS query is leaked to DNS
;; ->>HEADER<<- opcode: QUERY, status: NOERROR, id: 19147
;; flags: qr aa rd; QUERY: 1, ANSWER: 4, AUTHORITY: 0, ADDITIONAL: 5
;; WARNING: recursion requested but not available
```

```
;; OPT PSEUDOSECTION:
; EDNS: version: 0, flags:; udp: 4096
; COOKIE: e7a27f8ca0fb12eb (echoed)
;; QUESTION SECTION:
;_http._tcp.headless.default.svc.cluster.local. IN SRV


;; ANSWER SECTION:
_http._tcp.headless.default.svc.cluster.local. 5 IN SRV 0 25 80 10-5-104-3...
_http._tcp.headless.default.svc.cluster.local. 5 IN SRV 0 25 80 10-5-104-4...
_http._tcp.headless.default.svc.cluster.local. 5 IN SRV 0 25 80 10-5-105-3...
_http._tcp.headless.default.svc.cluster.local. 5 IN SRV 0 25 80 10-5-106-2...


;; ADDITIONAL SECTION:
10-5-104-4.headless.default.svc.cluster.local. 5 IN A 10.5.104.4
10-5-106-2.headless.default.svc.cluster.local. 5 IN A 10.5.106.2
10-5-104-3.headless.default.svc.cluster.local. 5 IN A 10.5.104.3
10-5-105-3.headless.default.svc.cluster.local. 5 IN A 10.5.105.3


;; Query time: 1 msec
;; SERVER: 10.7.240.9#53(10.7.240.9)
;; WHEN: Fri Mar 22 02:28:22 UTC 2019
;; MSG SIZE  rcvd: 770
```

The result's ANSWER SECTION includes an SRV record for each endpoint address, similar to the response for the A record request. However, the SRV also includes a priority, weight, port, and then the name for the A record corresponding to the endpoint address. In Kubernetes SRV records, the priority and weight are meaningless. But the port reflects the named port from the Service resource. The first label in the name, _http, corresponds to the port name "http," and the second label, _tcp, corresponds to the protocol field with "TCP." If there are multiple named ports, there will be SRV records for each endpoint and port combination. Unnamed ports from the Service do not get SRV records.

The ADDITIONAL SECTION of the result from the SRV query contains the A records referred to by the SRV record's targets. This allows them to be used immediately without any additional lookups for those names. The names used for these A records depend on the settings in the PodSpec for the underlying pod. If the PodSpec does not set a hostname and subdomain field or if the subdomain field does not match the name of this service, the first label will be an arbitrary unique identifier.[4] If those conditions are not true, then the hostname value will be used here.

---

4 By the specification, this could be anything. The older kube-dns uses an internal hash. CoreDNS uses the dashed version of the pod's IP address.

Example 6-6 shows an example of a Deployment resource with this setting in its pod template.

Example 6-6. Deployment with hostname and subdomain

```
apiVersion: apps/v1
kind: Deployment
metadata:
  name: headless
  namespace: default
spec:
  replicas: 4
  selector:
    matchLabels:
      app: headless
  template:
    metadata:
      labels:
        app: headless
    spec:
      hostname: myhost
      subdomain: headless
      containers:
      - image: nginx
        name: nginx
        ports:
        - containerPort: 80
          name: http
          protocol: TCP
```

The corresponding Service that we create to allow discovery of this service is still the one shown earlier in Example 6-2. Changing the Deployment's pod template does not require changes to the service. Example 6-7 shows what happens when we query for the SRV records of this service now that the hostname and subdomain are set.

Example 6-7. Headless service SRV records for Deployment with hostname and subdomain

```
dnstools# dig -t srv headless.default.svc.cluster.local


; <<>> DiG 9.11.3 <<>> -t srv headless.default.svc.cluster.local
;; global options: +cmd
;; Got answer:
;; WARNING: .local is reserved for Multicast DNS
;; You are currently testing what happens when an mDNS query is leaked to DNS
;; ->>HEADER<<- opcode: QUERY, status: NOERROR, id: 51823
;; flags: qr aa rd; QUERY: 1, ANSWER: 1, AUTHORITY: 0, ADDITIONAL: 5
;; WARNING: recursion requested but not available
```

```
;; OPT PSEUDOSECTION:
; EDNS: version: 0, flags:; udp: 4096
; COOKIE: b24f8ae8333bb0fa (echoed)
;; QUESTION SECTION:
;headless.default.svc.cluster.local. IN SRV


;; ANSWER SECTION:
headless.default.svc.cluster.local. 5 IN SRV 0 25 80 myhost.headless.default.svc...


;; ADDITIONAL SECTION:
myhost.headless.default.svc.cluster.local. 5 IN A 10.5.105.6
myhost.headless.default.svc.cluster.local. 5 IN A 10.5.105.5
myhost.headless.default.svc.cluster.local. 5 IN A 10.5.105.4
myhost.headless.default.svc.cluster.local. 5 IN A 10.5.105.7


;; Query time: 0 msec
;; SERVER: 10.7.240.9#53(10.7.240.9)
;; WHEN: Fri Mar 22 02:59:51 UTC 2019
;; MSG SIZE  rcvd: 412
```

Well, that's not really useful. Because a Deployment creates identical pods, you end up with a single name for all of the endpoints. This is functionally no different than just using the service name.

Where this feature is really important is when you are using a StatefulSet instead of a Deployment. A StatefulSet does not use the same hostname for each pod that it creates. Instead, it sets the hostname based on an ordinal number (0, 1, 2, etc.) and keeps this name even if the pod is deleted and recreated (a Deployment would generate a new pod name in this case). This provides a stable network identity for the pod. It also tracks any persistent volumes attached to the pod, and makes sure that the same volumes are mounted to the pod with the same name if a pod is destroyed (e.g., to reschedule it after a node dies).

Example 6-8 shows a StatefulSet resource. If you look closely, you will see that the PodSpec template does not actually contain the hostname and subdomain fields! When using the StatefulSet, the controller automatically generates the pod name and hostname, so there is no need to set it manually. In fact, if you do set it in the template, it will be ignored and overwritten by the controller. The serviceName field is used to tell the StatefulSet controller the value to use for the subdomain field.

Example 6-8. A StatefulSet

```
apiVersion: apps/v1
kind: StatefulSet
metadata:
  name: headless
  namespace: default
spec:
  replicas: 4
  serviceName: headless
  selector:
    matchLabels:
      app: headless
  template:
    metadata:
      labels:
        app: headless
    spec:
      containers:
      - image: nginx
        name: nginx
        ports:
        - containerPort: 80
          name: http
          protocol: TCP
```

The corresponding Service resource is identical to the one used for the Deployment example shown in Example 6-2. Example 6-9 shows what happens when we query for the SRV records corresponding to this service, now that it is backed by a StatefulSet instead of a Deployment.

Example 6-9. SRV records for a headless service and StatefulSet

```
dnstools# dig -t srv headless.default.svc.cluster.local


; <<>> DiG 9.11.3 <<>> -t srv headless.default.svc.cluster.local
;; global options: +cmd
;; Got answer:
;; WARNING: .local is reserved for Multicast DNS
;; You are currently testing what happens when an mDNS query is leaked to DNS
;; ->>HEADER<<- opcode: QUERY, status: NOERROR, id: 49617
;; flags: qr aa rd; QUERY: 1, ANSWER: 4, AUTHORITY: 0, ADDITIONAL: 5
;; WARNING: recursion requested but not available


;; OPT PSEUDOSECTION:
; EDNS: version: 0, flags:; udp: 4096
; COOKIE: 6a12b42776314007 (echoed)
;; QUESTION SECTION:
;headless.default.svc.cluster.local. IN SRV
```

```
;; ANSWER SECTION:
headless.default.svc.cluster.local. 5 IN SRV 0 25 80 headless-3.headless.default...
headless.default.svc.cluster.local. 5 IN SRV 0 25 80 headless-2.headless.default...
headless.default.svc.cluster.local. 5 IN SRV 0 25 80 headless-1.headless.default...
headless.default.svc.cluster.local. 5 IN SRV 0 25 80 headless-0.headless.default...


;; ADDITIONAL SECTION:
headless-2.headless.default.svc.cluster.local. 5 IN A 10.5.109.12
headless-0.headless.default.svc.cluster.local. 5 IN A 10.5.109.14
headless-1.headless.default.svc.cluster.local. 5 IN A 10.5.109.13
headless-3.headless.default.svc.cluster.local. 5 IN A 10.5.107.15


;; Query time: 1 msec
;; SERVER: 10.7.240.9#53(10.7.240.9)
;; WHEN: Fri Mar 22 23:50:19 UTC 2019
;; MSG SIZE  rcvd: 715
```

In this response, we see individual names for each endpoint. Even if we delete a pod so that the controller rebuilds it, we will see the same name, though the IP might change. Example 6-10 shows what happens when all of the pods are forcibly deleted. The controller relaunches the pods, just as it would for a Deployment. However, we see that it has kept a stable network identity for the pods. In fact, if we had attached persistent volumes to these pods as well, they would also be properly attached to the pod with the same name as before.

Example 6-10. Stable network identity using a StatefulSet

```
$ kubectl get po
NAME                     READY   STATUS    RESTARTS   AGE
headless-0               1/1     Running   0          14m
headless-1               1/1     Running   0          14m
headless-2               1/1     Running   0          14m
headless-3               1/1     Running   0          14m
$ kubectl delete po headless-{0,1,2,3} && kubectl get po
pod "headless-0" deleted
pod "headless-1" deleted
pod "headless-2" deleted
pod "headless-3" deleted


NAME                       READY   STATUS         RESTARTS   AGE
coredns-56c94cbf88-5tpvh   1/1     Running        0          1d
coredns-56c94cbf88-wcw4j   1/1     Running        0          3h
dnstools-5c98d9bbf-q9q25   1/1     Running        1          3h
headless-0                 1/1     Running        0          7s
headless-1                 1/1     Running        0          5s
```

```
headless-2                    1/1    Running             0       3s
headless-3                    0/1    ContainerCreating   0       0s
$ kubectl attach -it dnstools-5c98d9bbf-q9q25
Defaulting container name to dnstools.
Use 'kubectl describe pod/ -n default' to see all of the containers in this pod.
If you don't see a command prompt, try pressing enter.
dnstools# dig -t srv headless.default.svc.cluster.local @coredns


; <<>> DiG 9.11.3 <<>> -t srv headless.default.svc.cluster.local @coredns
;; global options: +cmd
;; Got answer:
;; WARNING: .local is reserved for Multicast DNS
;; You are currently testing what happens when an mDNS query is leaked to DNS
;; ->>HEADER<<- opcode: QUERY, status: NOERROR, id: 17599
;; flags: qr aa rd; QUERY: 1, ANSWER: 4, AUTHORITY: 0, ADDITIONAL: 5
;; WARNING: recursion requested but not available


;; OPT PSEUDOSECTION:
; EDNS: version: 0, flags:; udp: 4096
; COOKIE: 020bc7fabb2cdb8b (echoed)
;; QUESTION SECTION:
;headless.default.svc.cluster.local. IN SRV


;; ANSWER SECTION:
headless.default.svc.cluster.local. 5 IN SRV 0 25 80 headless-3.headless.default...
headless.default.svc.cluster.local. 5 IN SRV 0 25 80 headless-0.headless.default...
headless.default.svc.cluster.local. 5 IN SRV 0 25 80 headless-1.headless.default...
headless.default.svc.cluster.local. 5 IN SRV 0 25 80 headless-2.headless.default...


;; ADDITIONAL SECTION:
headless-0.headless.default.svc.cluster.local. 5 IN A 10.5.109.15
headless-1.headless.default.svc.cluster.local. 5 IN A 10.5.109.16
headless-3.headless.default.svc.cluster.local. 5 IN A 10.5.107.16
headless-2.headless.default.svc.cluster.local. 5 IN A 10.5.109.17


;; Query time: 1 msec
;; SERVER: 10.7.240.9#53(10.7.240.9)
;; WHEN: Fri Mar 22 23:57:33 UTC 2019
;; MSG SIZE  rcvd: 715
```

The specification also includes an A record for each pod, but this record is deprecated. The specification was written to represent existing kube-dns behavior, so these
records were included even if though they are no longer considered a best practice.
With these records, the DNS server will respond to queries of the form
a-b-c-d.namespace.pod.cluster.local, where a, b, c, and d are integers from 0 to
255 with an A record containing the IP a.b.c.d. There is no check for whether a pod

actually exists in the specified namespace with that IP address. The intention of this was for use with wildcard certificates (`*.namespace.pod.cluster.local.`); however, it weakens the guarantee of identity coming from DNS and thus weakens security. A bad actor might be able to use this automatic behavior to allow a pod outside the namespace to appear as one in the namespace to another service. Therefore, these records are deprecated in the specification.

That covers how DNS records in Kubernetes are designed to work in general. In the next section, we look at how CoreDNS is integrated with Kubernetes to make these records available to clients in the cluster.

CoreDNS Integration

Now we understand how services are created in Kubernetes and what DNS entries are used to find those services. But that still does not tell us how CoreDNS queries Kubernetes to provide responses to the DNS request. The CoreDNS kubernetes plug-in works very much like a controller, except that it never writes data back to the API server. It creates a watch on the Services and Endpoints resources, and caches that data. Whenever a request comes in for the plug-in to handle, it looks up whether that name corresponds to a resource, and returns the appropriate data if it does, as illustrated in Figure 6-1.

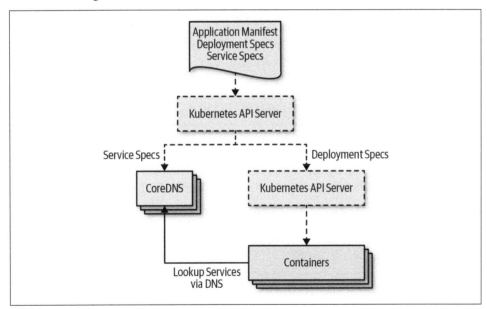

Figure 6-1. CoreDNS/Kubernetes integration

The response records are not generated and stored somewhere; they are built on the fly based on the incoming request. Because the Kubernetes resources are stored in an in-memory cache, building the records is very fast. By using the watch feature of the API server, these in-memory records stay up-to-date. CoreDNS never needs to query the API server in direct response to a DNS query, keeping DNS responses fast.

The in-memory cache of Kubernetes objects is completely unrelated to the DNS cache, which is enabled in CoreDNS with the cache plug-in. If CoreDNS is responding only to Kubernetes in-cluster requests, and not handling out-of-cluster queries to the larger network, there is very little benefit to enabling the cache plug-in. The cache plug-in keeps the resource records constructed by the kubernetes plug-in in memory by storing the response to the DNS query. Even though returning those records may be slightly faster than reconstructing them, there is additional overhead for hashing and retrieving the data, minimizing any performance gain for cache hits, while degrading performance in the cache-miss case.

The kubernetes plug-in watches both Services and Endpoints. Services are required to provide responses to queries for clusterIP services, and Endpoints are required to reply to headless service queries. If you do not need to support headless services (which often are also used in conjunction with StatefulSets), you can disable the Endpoints watch by using the plug-in option noendpoints.

Why would you want to do that? The Endpoints structure in Kubernetes is troublesome. The resource itself is called Endpoints—plural—because a single Endpoints resource contains all of the endpoint addresses, both ready and not, for a single service. For a service with a lot of backends, this can be a very large data structure. Not only that, but recall that *watch* will send the resource data *whenever the resource changes*. For Endpoints, this means that every time a pod for the specific service is create, destroyed, or transitions between ready and not ready, the entire Endpoints object will be sent.

The more backends a service has, the larger the Endpoints object (the more addresses in it), and the more likely one of those backends changes. This means that larger Endpoints are sent to watchers more often than smaller Endpoints, resulting in scaling challenges for very large services containing several thousand backends. Large services will cause CoreDNS to consume substantially more memory and CPU than small services.[5] If you do not need headless services, disabling the Endpoints watch will help keep resource use down.

---

5 Worse, etcd has a limit to the size of objects that can be stored. If the number of backends grows too high, the list of addresses will be truncated. Because the ordering of the addresses is not deterministic, the truncation might leave out different addresses each time through the reconciliation loop of the Endpoints controller, causing even more churn.

Now that we understand how the kubernetes plug-in works, we need to see how it is configured. In fact, the kubernetes plug-in is just part of the CoreDNS configuration that is typically deployed in Kubernetes. In the next section, we go into detail about the common, default CoreDNS configuration used in Kubernetes, including other plug-in configurations.

Default Configuration

You can create Kubernetes clusters in many different ways, and it is up to the person creating the cluster to specify the exact configuration of each component, including CoreDNS. To make this easier, there are many different deployment tools, such as kubeadm, kube-spray, or minikube, and each tool takes responsibility for creating all of the Kubernetes resources needed by the cluster. This includes the CoreDNS *Corefile*. In theory, each of these tools can determine exactly what they want the *Corefile* to contain. However, in practice, most follow the recommendations of the CoreDNS team.

The CoreDNS GitHub organization has a *deployment* repository that contains the recommendations of the CoreDNS team in the *kubernetes* directory at *https:// github.com/coredns/deployment/tree/master/kubernetes*. Most of the tools use this configuration with only small changes for their specific workflows. The version of the recommended *Corefile* as of this writing is shown in Example 6-11.

Example 6-11. Kubernetes Corefile

```
.:53 {
    errors
    health
    kubernetes CLUSTER_DOMAIN REVERSE_CIDRS {
      pods insecure
      upstream
      fallthrough in-addr.arpa ip6.arpa
    }
    prometheus :9153
    forward . UPSTREAMNAMESERVER
    cache 30
    loop
    reload
    loadbalance
}
```

We will go through this file in detail to understand why each line is here. One thing to note is that the values in ALL_CAPS are variables that are replaced by the deployment tools that process this file; for example, by kubeadm. Kubernetes itself does not understand or do anything with these, and if you were to use this file directly as is, you would break your CoreDNS deployment in Kubernetes.

As described in Chapter 3, the first line, `.:53 {`, starts a new server block for the server running on port 53 and instructs that server to resolve queries for the root domain and everything underneath it (i.e., any domain). This means that all queries will be passed through the set of plug-ins listed in this server block, unless there is another, more specific server block that matches the query (e.g., see "Stub Domains and Federations" on page 96).

The next line, `errors`, enables the `errors` plug-in. This plug-in logs any errors returned during query processing. These include errors such as networking timeouts to upstream name servers. This plug-in affects only whether the errors are logged, not the actual DNS response code. Without this plug-in, CoreDNS will still respond with a SERVFAIL in most of these cases, but will log nothing. Troubleshooting is much easier when errors are logged.

The `health` plug-in exposes a health-check endpoint for the kubelet to monitor whether CoreDNS is alive and functioning. It opens an HTTP server on port 8080, which will respond to an HTTP request for `/health`. It is configured as a kubelet health check as described in "Cluster DNS Deployment Resources" on page 98.

The third line, `kubernetes CLUSTER_DOMAIN REVERSE_CIDRS {`, enables the `kubernetes` plug-in, giving it authority over the `CLUSTER_DOMAIN`—in our example, this is `cluster.example.com`. It also needs to be able to respond to PTR requests for services running in the cluster, so `REVERSE_CIDRS` should be populated with the Kubernetes service Classless Inter-Domain Routing (CIDR). For example, if your service CIDR is 10.7.240.0/20, you would use this value for `REVERSE_CIDR`. If you also want to resolve PTR queries for service endpoints, you also need all pod CIDRs in this list. Because service and pod CIDRs are not discoverable via the Kubernetes API, CoreDNS cannot figure these out on its own. Alternatively, you can specify `in-addr.arpa` and `ipv6.arpa`, and all reverse DNS requests will be considered by the plug-in.

Inside the `kubernetes` plug-in configuration block, three different features are enabled. The `pods insecure` line provides support for a deprecated part of the DNS specification that responds to a special form of query for pod IP addresses. This is provided for backward compatibility with the prior default cluster DNS solution, kube-dns. If you do not need this, you should remove this line; more detail on the `pods` configuration is available in "CoreDNS Extensions" on page 111.

The `upstream` line instructs the plug-in to resolve canonical name (CNAME) records by sending queries back to CoreDNS itself. CNAMEs are used when a service is defined with `type: ExternalName` instead of `type: ClusterIP`. The `upstream` option allows the stub domain and other settings to be honored, and it also allows CNAMEs that resolve to services within the cluster. This line is unnecessary in versions 1.4 and later of CoreDNS; it is the default behavior in those versions.

The last `kubernetes` plug-in configuration is `fallthrough in-addr.arpa ip6.arp`. This instructs the plug-in that if it does not find a record when doing a PTR lookup, it should pass the request down the plug-in chain. This is especially important when you do not explicitly list all of the service and pod CIDRs in the *Corefile*, because in that case the configuration normally would send all PTR requests through the `kubernetes` plug-in. Without this `fallthrough` line, the plug-in would swallow any PTR request for any IP; with the line here, it passes unknown IPs down the chain where they will be picked up by the `forward` plug-in.

After the `kubernetes` plug-in, the line `prometheus :9153` appears. This enables the `prometheus` plug-in, which exports metrics for scraping by Prometheus. By default, the `prometheus` plug-in listens only on localhost, to prevent accidental exposure to potentially sensitive metrics. By specifying `:9153`, we are instructing it to listen on all addresses on port 9153. Because Prometheus scrapes the metrics from across the network, this is necessary to make them accessible.

The `forward . UPSTREAMNAMESERVER` line appears next. It enables the `forward` plug-in for the root zone ("."). Any queries received by this server that are not handled by an earlier plug-in will be forwarded to the nameserver(s) specified. One important thing to note is that "earlier" does not refer to "listed earlier in the Corefile." As described in Chapter 3, queries are processed through plug-ins in a fixed order, determined at compile time. The order in the *Corefile* is not relevant across plug-ins, although for plug-ins that allow multiple instances within a server block, the order is significant.

The `cache 30` line enables the `cache` plug-in, capping the time-to-live (TTL) of records at 30 seconds. The actual TTL used for a given record will be the *lesser* of the record's configured TTL and the cache's configured TTL. The use of the cache here is not ideal. It is useful for upstream requests, but any requests for inside the cluster domain do not gain much value from the cache. The `kubernetes` plug-in itself already holds all of the Kubernetes resources in memory, so the additional caching is not necessary. We resolve this in "A Better Configuration" on page 106.

The `loop` plug-in is enabled next, via the `loop` directive. This is a defensive plug-in that is used to detect DNS query loops. If a loop is detected, CoreDNS will exit with an error log entry explaining the issue. Although it might seem severe to exit, it ensures that the loop is dealt with. This prevents intermittent, very-difficult-to-debug DNS failures.

The `reload` directive enables the `reload` plug-in, which allows CoreDNS to reload its *Corefile* without having to restart the process. This means that you can simply `kubectl -n kube-system edit configmap coredns`, and any changes you make will automatically be reloaded. When you change a `ConfigMap`, it can take a minute or two to propagate the change to all the nodes that need it. CoreDNS will check the

MD5 checksum periodically (every 30s by default) and reload the file if it has changed.

 Reload Can Be Dangerous

Be sure to test any changes in a lab or duplicate deployment first! If there is a syntax error in the *Corefile*, CoreDNS will log an error and continue to serve with the original *Corefile*. If the CoreDNS pod is killed or later rescheduled to another node, the newly started process will read the erroneous Corefile and be unable to start.

Finally, the `loadbalance` directive enables the `loadbalance` plug-in, which simply randomly shuffles A/AAAA records in the response. When using headless services, this means that different clients will receive the records in a different order. Because many clients simply take the first IP returned, this helps spread the load across all instances.

That covers the essential configuration of CoreDNS for Kubernetes. For clarity, we did omit a few details, in particular about configuring stub domains and federations. These are covered in the next section.

Stub Domains and Federations

If you look at the *Corefile* in the GitHub repository, shown in Example 6-12, you will notice a couple of other variables that are substituted when generating the final *Corefile*: STUBDOMAINS and FEDERATIONS. These were left out of the first listing of this file to focus on the more commonly used variables.

Example 6-12. Kubernetes Corefile with all variables

```
.:53 {
    errors
    health
    kubernetes CLUSTER_DOMAIN REVERSE_CIDRS {
      pods insecure
      upstream
      fallthrough in-addr.arpa ip6.arpa
    }FEDERATIONS
    prometheus :9153
    forward . UPSTREAMNAMESERVER
    cache 30
    loop
    reload
    loadbalance
}STUBDOMAINS
```

The STUBDOMAINS variable is used to populate additional server stanzas when you want to resolve specific domains using name servers other than UPSTREAMNAME SERVER. This is typically used to resolve local domains using an internal DNS server, as shown in Example 6-13.

Example 6-13. Corefile for Kubernetes with stub domain

```
.:53 {
    errors
    health
    kubernetes cluster.local in-addr.arpa ip6.arpa {
      pods insecure
      upstream
      fallthrough in-addr.arpa ip6.arpa
    }
    prometheus :9153
    forward . /etc/resolv.conf
    cache 30
    loop
    reload
    loadbalance
}

corp.example.com:53 {
    errors
    cache 30
    loop
    forward . 10.0.0.10:53
}
```

In this example, queries for anything under corp.example.com go through the second server block because queries are directed through the server block with the longest match. These are then forwarded to a local name server at 10.0.0.10 rather than through the name servers defined in */etc/resolv.conf.*

The FEDERATIONS variable is used to support Kubernetes federation v1 names. It enables the federation plug-in, and allows specification of the federated zones. Federation v1 was a control plane for managing workloads across multiple clusters, but it is no longer in active development. The federation plug-in is provided for backward compatibility, and it will be removed in a future version. There are several other multiple-cluster management projects being explored by the Kubernetes community, including a federation v2. Any support for these will be built as external plug-ins to start.

The *Corefile* describes how CoreDNS behaves when running as cluster DNS, but there are many other resources needed to manage and deploy your CoreDNS in your cluster. The next section describes those resources.

Cluster DNS Deployment Resources

The deployment GitHub repository also contains the Kubernetes resource definitions necessary to get CoreDNS up and running. This includes how it accesses the API server, the container image used, the number of pods to run, and other deployment details. This section details all of the Kubernetes resources contained in the manifests in the deployment repository.

There are four categories of resources needed for CoreDNS to run: CoreDNS needs resources that grant it access to the API server, a ConfigMap to hold its *Corefile*, a Service to make DNS available to the cluster, and a Deployment to actually launch and manage its pods. The ConfigMap was covered in "Default Configuration" on page 93, so next we look at the other categories. We begin with the Kubernetes resources needed for CoreDNS to access the API server.

Role-Based Access Control

CoreDNS needs access to the API server in order to read service and endpoint data. By default, pods in Kubernetes are given access to a service account token that can be used to query the API server. This default token typically has access to only the same namespace in which the pod is running. For CoreDNS to be able to read data from the API server for all services cluster-wide, it requires a service account with broader access.

For this reason, the default manifests used to deploy CoreDNS for in-cluster DNS creates the Role-Based Access Control (RBAC) resources. The simplest of these is the coredns service account, shown in Example 6-14. This just creates a named account that can be referred to later, when creating the Deployment. The PodSpec will be configured to use this named service account.

Example 6-14. CoreDNS ServiceAccount

```
apiVersion: v1
kind: ServiceAccount
metadata:
  name: coredns
  namespace: kube-system
```

To grant privileges to this service account, a role is needed; in this case, the Cluster Role as shown in Example 6-15. A ClusterRole, as opposed to a Role, is not tied to any specific namespace. Because CoreDNS needs to read data across all namespaces, we must use a ClusterRole.

Example 6-15. CoreDNS ClusterRole

```
apiVersion: rbac.authorization.k8s.io/v1
kind: ClusterRole
metadata:
  labels:
    kubernetes.io/bootstrapping: rbac-defaults
  name: system:coredns
rules:
- apiGroups:
  - ""
  resources:
  - endpoints
  - services
  - pods
  - namespaces
  verbs:
  - list
  - watch
- apiGroups:
  - ""
  resources:
  - nodes
  verbs:
  - get
```

The `ClusterRole` is useless, however, until we associate it with the service account. This is the purpose of the `ClusterRoleBinding`, as shown in Example 6-16. It assigns the role to the specific service account, so that Kubernetes will grant the role's privileges to any client connecting with that service account.

Example 6-16. CoreDNS ClusterRoleBinding

```
apiVersion: rbac.authorization.k8s.io/v1
kind: ClusterRoleBinding
metadata:
  annotations:
    rbac.authorization.kubernetes.io/autoupdate: "true"
  labels:
    kubernetes.io/bootstrapping: rbac-defaults
  name: system:coredns
roleRef:
  apiGroup: rbac.authorization.k8s.io
  kind: ClusterRole
  name: system:coredns
subjects:
- kind: ServiceAccount
  name: coredns
  namespace: kube-system
```

Let's take a closer look at the `ClusterRole`. It grants the ability to *list* and *watch* any of the resources Endpoints, Services, pods, and namespaces. It also grants the ability to *get* nodes. Based on the DNS specification, the ability to watch and list Endpoints and Services makes sense: it needs those resources to construct the records for clusterIP and headless services. But does it need pods, namespaces, and nodes?

There are a couple reasons it needs access to namespaces. The first is to decide whether to return `NXDOMAIN` or `SUCCESS` with no data when a query comes in for `name space.svc.cluster.local`. To properly implement DNS, CoreDNS cannot return `NXDOMAIN` for this name if names exist within that subdomain; that is, if any services exist in the namespace. Namespace records are also necessary when using wildcard queries, which are a CoreDNS extension described in "Wildcard Queries" on page 112.

The answer for whether it needs pods and nodes is "probably not." There are a number of optional features that might be enabled in the *Corefile* that would require this access, but the default *Corefile* does not enable those features. The CoreDNS authors chose to recommend granting these privileges to avoid complicating the deployment instructions. This way, changes to the cluster role are not needed if the features are enabled in the *Corefile*. If you are not using any of those features, you can remove those extra privileges.

CoreDNS needs to watch pods only if you enable the `pods verified` option, described in "Pod Options" on page 111. If this is not enabled, there is no need to keep the privilege to read pods.

Now that you understand how CoreDNS will access the API server, let's look at how clients will find and access CoreDNS over the network by examining the Service defined in the deployment scripts.

Service

CoreDNS uses a standard Cluster IP service, like those discussed in "Cluster IP Services" on page 80. The specific Service as defined in the manifest is shown in Example 6-17.

Example 6-17. The kube-dns service

```
apiVersion: v1
kind: Service
metadata:
  name: coredns
  labels:
    app: coredns
spec:
  selector:
```

```
    app: coredns
  clusterIP: 10.7.240.10
  ports:
  - name: dns
    port: 53
    protocol: UDP
  - name: dns-tcp
    port: 53
    protocol: TCP
  - name: metrics
    port: 9153
    protocol: TCP
```

The first thing that you might notice is that the service is named "kube-dns" instead of "coredns." The service name is the same, regardless of the DNS service provider. In earlier versions of Kubernetes, kube-dns was also the name of the DNS server. However, to provide a seamless upgrade—without loss of service—from that server to CoreDNS, it was necessary to keep the service name the same. In Kubernetes, the name and clusterIP of a Service are immutable. Thus, changing the service name would have required deleting the service and recreating it with a different name, or changing the clusterIP. Either of these options would have caused an interruption of service.

In the example, the clusterIP is 10.7.240.10, but this will vary with the cluster. It will be a fixed value determined at the creation time of the cluster, and will not be auto-allocated by Kubernetes. The same IP address is passed into each instance of the kubelet, which will use it when creating the *resolv.conf* file for the pods that it launches.

The service defines three named ports. The first two are the Transmission Control Protocol (TCP) and User Datagram Protocol (UDP) ports for DNS, as expected. The third is the metrics port, which defines the port used by Prometheus to scrape metrics. The strange thing here, though, is that Prometheus needs to scrape from each individual *instance* of CoreDNS. It doesn't make sense to scrape from the service, because the values retrieved will be from a different backend each time. So why is this defined? In fact, Prometheus uses the service to identify the port to use for scraping the pods, but does not actually scrape the pods *through* the service. Instead, it scrapes the pods directly, but using the port defined in the service.

This leaves us with one more resource: the Deployment.

Deployment

The YAML definition of the Deployment resource is very long, so rather than listing it all, we will take a look at it piece by piece. It of course begins with the standard fields: a kind Deployment from the apps/v1 apiVersion group and metadata.name "coredns." The interesting bit begins in the `spec` field, the first part of which is shown in Example 6-18.

Example 6-18. CoreDNS Deployment—part 1

```
spec:
  replicas: 2
  strategy:
    type: RollingUpdate
    rollingUpdate:
      maxUnavailable: 1
  selector:
    matchLabels:
      app: coredns
```

In this section, the default number of replicas (2) is specified. In most deployments, the number of replicas is adjusted by the cluster-proportional autoscaler. This is a separate Deployment that runs and scales the number of CoreDNS replicas based on the number of nodes in the cluster. For more on autoscaling CoreDNS, see "Autoscaling" on page 105.

The next field, the strategy field, defines how to update pods in the deployment when a change is made that requires restarting pods. That could be an image update to a new version of CoreDNS, or it could be a change to other parameters such as the requested resources or resource limits. Using the `RollingUpdate` strategy with a value of `1` for `maxUnavailable` will take down a single replica and replace it, waiting until it is running successfully before moving on to the next replica.

Finally, the `selector` field defines how the Deployment identifies pods that are under its control.

The remainder of the Deployment resource consists of the pod template. The first part of this is shown in Example 6-19. It starts by simply defining the labels to apply to the pods, such that they match the deployment selector. After that it sets the `serviceAccountName` to the coredns service account that was described in Example 6-14, defines a single volume for the pod that contains the *Corefile*, and specifies the `dnsPolicy` as `Default`.

Painfully, the `dnsPolicy` called "Default" is not the default for pods. The default for pods is `ClusterFirst`—which means to use the kube-dns service as the DNS name server for the pod. The `Default` policy actually means to use the host node's DNS configuration. CoreDNS uses this policy so that it can resolve external names using the configured upstream name servers for the node.

Example 6-19. CoreDNS Deployment—part 2

```
template:
  metadata:
    labels:
      app: coredns
  spec:
    serviceAccountName: coredns
    volumes:
      - name: config-volume
        configMap:
          name: coredns
          items:
          - key: Corefile
            path: Corefile
    dnsPolicy: Default
```

The final part of the pod template for this deployment resource is the list of containers. CoreDNS pods have only a single container, the definition for which is shown in Example 6-20. This container runs a single process: the CoreDNS instance itself. Caching, health, and metrics are implemented as plug-ins. In the earlier kube-dns implementation, these different functions ran as separate processes.

The first part of the CoreDNS container specification simply defines the name and image to use, and how to mount the *Corefile* from the `ConfigMap` and consume it. It defines the TCP and UDP ports for DNS, and the TCP port for use by Prometheus to scrape metrics.

Example 6-20. CoreDNS Deployment—part 3

```
      containers:
      - name: coredns
        image: coredns/coredns:1.3.1
        imagePullPolicy: IfNotPresent
        args: [ "-conf", "/etc/coredns/Corefile" ]
        volumeMounts:
        - name: config-volume
          mountPath: /etc/coredns
          readOnly: true
        ports:
        - containerPort: 53
          name: dns
          protocol: UDP
        - containerPort: 53
          name: dns-tcp
          protocol: TCP
        - containerPort: 9153
          name: metrics
          protocol: TCP
        resources:
```

```
      limits:
        memory: 170Mi
      requests:
        cpu: 100m
        memory: 70Mi
    securityContext:
      allowPrivilegeEscalation: false
      capabilities:
        add:
        - NET_BIND_SERVICE
        drop:
        - all
      readOnlyRootFilesystem: true
    livenessProbe:
      httpGet:
        path: /health
        port: 8080
        scheme: HTTP
      initialDelaySeconds: 60
      timeoutSeconds: 5
      successThreshold: 1
      failureThreshold: 5
    readinessProbe:
      httpGet:
        path: /health
        port: 8080
        scheme: HTTP
```

Next come the resource limits. For this, CoreDNS requests a minimum of one-tenth of a CPU, but does not put a limit on the CPU consumption. CoreDNS is CPU bound, so this allows it to scale to the available CPUs on the node. With memory, it is important to set a limit because a process consuming too much memory on the node can cause the kernel to start killing processes. If a process consumes too much CPU, things will slow down but it won't cause crashing.

The limit of 170 Mi (mebibytes) of memory was the same amount as set for the original kube-dns container; when upgrading to CoreDNS, keeping this the same ensures that a cluster will be able to schedule the same number of CoreDNS pods as there were kube-dns pods. Scale testing showed that CoreDNS is able to keep within this memory limit when handling a 5,000-node cluster.

Memory Limit Estimation

To estimate the limit needed for your cluster with the default *Corefile* settings, use this estimate:

$$\text{MiB needed} = (\text{pods} + \text{Services}) / 1000 + 54$$

So, for a cluster with 10,000 pods and 6,000 services, the limit can be set to $(10,000 + 6,000) / 1,000 + 54 = 16 + 54 = 70$ MiB.

The security context defined for CoreDNS sets NET_BIND_SERVICE, and drops all other process capabilities. This allows CoreDNS to run as a nonroot user, but still bind to a port less than 1024 (i.e., to the DNS port 53).

Finally, readiness and liveness probes are defined. They both call the health plug-in, but Kubernetes uses these for different purposes. When the liveness probe fails (takes more than timeoutSeconds) five times, the CoreDNS process is killed and restarted. Passing the readiness probe, on the other hand, allows the CoreDNS process to receive traffic by adding it to the clusterIP load-balancing pool. Newer versions of CoreDNS have separate health and ready plug-ins.

So, that's all there is to how CoreDNS is deployed in Kubernetes...almost. These resources completely define the initial deployment of CoreDNS. If you have a static cluster, that is all you need. However, many clusters change in size over time. The next section describes how to set up autoscaling for CoreDNS in Kubernetes.

Autoscaling

As we saw in Example 6-18, by default only two replicas of CoreDNS are deployed. That is fine for a small cluster, but in a larger cluster, you will need many more replicas. To handle that, many distributions will deploy a dns-autoscaler pod. This pod is based on the general-purpose cluster-proportional autoscaler. It will add new replicas as the number of cores or nodes in the cluster increases. By default, it will always maintain at least two replicas, and will set the replicas such that there is one per 256 cores or one per 16 nodes in the cluster, whichever is larger.

Cluster size is a very rough way to estimate how many DNS instances are needed. The actual need will vary depending on the workloads you are running on your cluster. In this deployment, CoreDNS is CPU bound. This means that autoscaling based on CPU using the standard Kubernetes Horizontal Pod Autoscaler (HPA) is an option. Example 6-21 presents a sample HPA resource. The maximum number of replicas is a required field; you should set it to something that will not put strain on your cluster.

Example 6-21. Horizontal Pod Autoscaler

```
apiVersion: autoscaling/v1
kind: HorizontalPodAutoscaler
metadata:
  name: coredns
  namespace: default
spec:
  maxReplicas: 20
  minReplicas: 2
  scaleTargetRef:
    apiVersion: apps/v1
    kind: Deployment
```

```
  name: coredns
targetCPUUtilizationPercentage: 50
```

In kube-dns, which had three separate processes running per pod, it was a bit difficult to understand what an aggregated CPU reading meant with respect to actual query performance. But with CoreDNS, there is only a single process, so it is clear that if it is struggling, more replicas should help. In this case, we target a CPU utilization of 50%, leaving capacity to give the autoscaler time to make adjustments or to handle short bursts of queries.

Kubernetes can also scale on metrics other than CPU. CoreDNS publishes a metric called `coredns_health_request_duration_seconds`, which measures how long CoreDNS takes to respond to the requests sent to the `health` plug-in. Because the `health` plug-in response is completely internal, this should be an extremely fast operation. If it is not, CoreDNS is struggling to handle the query load. You can use this as a signal to add more CoreDNS instances using autoscaling.

Now you fully understand all of the basics of how CoreDNS integrates with Kubernetes, the standard configuration for CoreDNS, and how it is deployed and scaled in Kubernetes. Next, we can go beyond these basics, and look at ways that we might be able to improve the functioning and performance of CoreDNS, depending on the specifics of an individual cluster. We will start by seeing if we can improve on the standard configuration.

A Better Configuration

As we went through the standard configuration line-by-line, we pointed out a few things that could be done better. One is that the `cache` plug-in is really redundant for in-cluster names because the underlying Kubernetes resources are already in memory. We do still want the cache to apply to out-of-cluster queries, though. To fix that, we could use a *Corefile*, as shown in Example 6-22.

Example 6-22. A better Kubernetes Corefile—step 1

```
CLUSTER_DOMAIN REVERSE_CIDRS {
    errors
    health
    kubernetes {
      pods insecure
      upstream
      fallthrough in-addr.arpa ip6.arpa
    }
    prometheus :9153
    forward . UPSTREAMNAMESERVER
    loop
```

```
        reload
        loadbalance
}

. {
        errors
        forward . UPSTREAMNAMESERVER
        prometheus :9153
        cache
        loop
}
```

By moving the CLUSTER_DOMAIN and REVERSE_CIDRS to the beginning of the server block, we are telling CoreDNS that it should route queries for those zones only through this set of plug-ins, which does not include the cache plug-in. Queries for other zones will go through the second stanza, and so will be cached. Because the queries coming through this server block are not for cluster services, we can let them be cached according to their upstream TTLs, so we remove the 30-second cap on that cache.[6]

Moving the CLUSTER_DOMAIN and REVERSE_CIDRS to the beginning of the server block does have a downside, though. For each zone listed at the front of the server block, CoreDNS will create an independent plug-in chain. This means that the Kubernetes caches will be duplicated within the CoreDNS instance, increasing the memory consumption. If you do not have a large cluster, this is neglible. But for larger clusters, you will need to make a decision about the trade-off between the small latency hit of having an extra cache plug-in check, and the memory used by having multiple kubernetes plug-ins loaded. There is ongoing work to resolve this, but it likely will not be completed before CoreDNS 1.7.0.

Notice that the health and reload plug-ins are not enabled in the second server block. The reload plug-in is a global option, so it needs to be listed only once in any *Corefile*. For versions 1.5.0 and later, the health plug-in is also global. Earlier versions asked plug-ins if they were healthy and reported back an aggregated status. This resulted in some production issues, so the simpler global health was adopted. The ready plug-in, also added in 1.5.0, allows per-plug-in readiness, which is what we need for Kubernetes.

This *Corefile* is better, but there are still some ways we can improve, such as adding the ready plug-in. We add it only to the first server block because we want to indicate readiness as soon as the Kubernetes API caches are full. Because pod records are deprecated and will be removed from the specification in the future, we do not want to

---

6 In fact, that is really only useful in the original *Corefile* for making sure negative responses are only cached for 30s, instead of based on the start of authority (SOA) record's TTL.

encourage their use in any new deployments. So, unless there is a specific reason we need it in our cluster, we can pull out the pods insecure line. That makes it a tiny bit better.

What about the forward plug-in? Do we still need that? The answer is "maybe." We want the *kubernetes* plug-in to handle reverse zones for the cluster service CIDR and the cluster pod CIDRs. If we cannot definitively list all of those CIDRs, we need to list a larger CIDR that contains them all, or we need to list the entire in-addr.arpa and ip6.arpa[7] zones. However, if we list those larger zones, the queries for many IPs that do not fall under the control of Kubernetes will come through this server block. If we do not include the fallthrough in-addr.arpa ip6.arpa and the forward . UPSTREAMNAMESERVER, PTR queries for those IPs will be handled by the kubernetes plug-in, which will return *NXDOMAIN*.

If we can enumerate those CIDRs, we can remove both of those lines. If we further assume that we are using CoreDNS 1.4 or later, the upstream line is redundant given that this is the default behavior in those versions of CoreDNS. This results in the *Corefile* presented in Example 6-23.

Example 6-23. A better Kubernetes Corefile—step 2

```
CLUSTER_DOMAIN REVERSE_CIDRS {
    errors
    health
    kubernetes
    ready
    prometheus :9153
    loop
    reload
    loadbalance
}

. {
    errors
    forward . UPSTREAMNAMESERVER
    cache
    loop
}
```

This is simpler, and it is also more operationally efficient. We could take it a step further and enable the autopath plug-in to alleviate the query magnification effect described in "Autopath and the Dreaded ndots:5" on page 113. However, this makes sense only if the cluster is not large and does a lot of lookups of external DNS names.

___

7 IPv6 is coming to Kubernetes. Any day now.

For autopath to work, it requires a watch on pods (pods verified mode), which can require a lot of memory and put excessive load on the API server if there are a lot of frequently changing pods.

This *Corefile* works for the standard Kubernetes service discovery. The kubernetes plug-in also offers the ability to deviate from that standard if you need to for special purposes. In the next section, we cover all the various options for the kubernetes plug-in.

The kubernetes Plug-in

At the heart of the integration of CoreDNS and Kubernetes is the kubernetes plug-in. The complete syntax for this plug-in allows for a number of different uses cases than the standard deployment we have discussed in this chapter. Some of these include the ability to run CoreDNS outside the cluster and access the API server as an external client, filtering of records by namespace or label selector, DNS zone transfers, and various tweaks to the way records are presented to client. Here is the complete syntax for the plug-in:

```
kubernetes [ZONES...] {
    resyncperiod DURATION
    endpoint URL
    tls CERT KEY CACERT
    kubeconfig KUBECONFIG CONTEXT
    namespaces NAMESPACE...
    labels EXPRESSION
    pods POD-MODE
    endpoint_pod_names
    noendpoints
    ignore empty_service
    ttl TTL
    upstream [ADDRESS...]
    transfer to ADDRESS...
    fallthrough [ZONES...]
}
```

Following is a description of each of the optional configuration keys:

resyncperiod

    Defines how often a resync[8] of the resources from the API server should be performed. The default is 5 minutes in versions before 1.5.0, and never in 1.5.0 and later. This option will be eliminated in later versions.

---

8 This terminology comes from the Kubernetes API client libraries. A resync is not the same as "relist and reload everything"; it is an internal-only process used to help rectify bugs in some early clients. It is no longer needed.

endpoint

Allows you to specify a specific API server URL to use. This is primarily used when running outside of Kubernetes.

tls

Used with endpoint to configure the TLS client parameters, as described in "tls" on page 50.

kubeconfig

Allows you to use a standard *kubeconfig* file to authenticate to the API server. This is intended to be used outside of Kubernetes. CoreDNS will connect to the API server defined in the CONTEXT listed. As of version 1.5.0, CoreDNS supports client certificates, bearer tokens, HTTP Basic authentication, as well as the GCP, OpenStack, and OIDC plug-ins.

namespaces *and* **labels**

Allow selectively exposing services, as described in "Modifying the Available Records" on page 117.

pods

Used to modify how pod queries are handled; see "Pod Options" on page 111 for details.

endpoint_pod_names

Changes how endpoint names are determined; see "Modifying the Available Records" on page 117.

noendpoints

Disables endpoint records altogether.

ignore empty_service

Treats a service with no backends as if it does not exist, returning NXDOMAIN instead of simply returning no data. Note that there is a space after ignore; this is to enable future extensions on what to ignore.

ttl

Controls the TTL used for all names related to cluster resources. It does not affect the TTL of records from upstream name servers.

upstream

Used for looking up the A record corresponding to CNAME records. It is obsolete in CoreDNS 1.3.0 and later because those versions always look up the A records internally.

`transfer to`
Controls the zone transfer feature described in "Zone Transfer Support" on page 115.

`fallthrough`
Allows queries for the listed zones to be passed down the plug-in chain to later plug-ins, as described in "fallthrough" on page 50. This will often be used to pass PTR requests upstream for all `in-addr.arpa` because there is no way to programatically figure out all of the CIDRs for endpoints.

In the next section, we describe in more detail how the pod options work, along with other special CoreDNS features for Kubernetes.

CoreDNS Extensions

CoreDNS offers options that go beyond the Kubernetes DNS specification. These are described in the subsections that follow. Use these with care, as some of them can cause your cluster to be nonconforming and affect workload portability.

Pod Options

As described in "Kubernetes DNS Specification" on page 82, the "pod" records are deprecated. CoreDNS offers three choices for handling pod name requests. The default for CoreDNS is `pods disabled`; if you omit the pods option, pod queries will return `NXDOMAIN`. For the default Kubernetes configuration, `pods insecure` is used, which maintains the deprecated but backward-compatible behavior of kube-dns.

The third option is `pods verified`. With this option, CoreDNS will initiate a watch on pod resources and will return an IP address only for the query `a-b-c-d.namespace.pod.cluster.local` if there is actually a pod in the specified namespace with IP address `a.b.c.d`. This prevents pods outside the namespace from appearing as if they are in the namespace, which improves security.[9]

The `pods verified` option is not enabled by default, because in large clusters, it introduces two scalability issues. The first is on the API server. Each individual CoreDNS instance puts a separate watch on the API server. The more pods you have, the more each watch affects the API server performance, and the more CoreDNS instances you need. This creates a nonlinear hit to API server load as the number of pods increases.

---

9 Allowing it to appear as if a pod outside a namespace is actually in a namespace weakens any DNS-based identity guarantees when using TLS; thus, the "insecure" moniker.

Enabling `pods verified` also increases the memory required by CoreDNS. Each instance must cache all pods in addition to services and endpoints. For a cluster with 25,000 pods and 1,000 services, CoreDNS will consume about 160 MiB in `pods verified` mode, and 80 MiB with `pods insecure` or `pods disabled`. For a cluster with 50,000 pods and 2,000 services, those numbers are 264 MiB and 106 MiB, respectively. Memory use is linear with the number of pods and services; see Memory Limit Estimation.

Technically, turning off `pods insecure` is not part of the Kubernetes DNS specification. However, the risk is low for damaging portability in this case because those records are deprecated.

Wildcard Queries

The `kubernetes` plug-in supports wildcard queries similar to the original SkyDNS and the etcd plug-in. This is completely separate and distinct from the concept of wildcard records in DNS. It is a special feature added to aid in service discovery.

Wildcard queries simply allow you to use a `*` or the word `all` as a label for certain parts of the name. When you do that, records will be returned regardless of what is in that label in the server. Example 6-24 shows an example, querying for all of the services in a particular namespace. Notice that the returned records do not have a name matching the actual service; instead, the name matches the one used in the query. Many clients will reject answers if the name in the answer does not match the name in the query.

Example 6-24. Wildcard query for all services in a namespace

```
dnstools# host *.default.svc.cluster.local.
*.default.svc.cluster.local has address 10.7.240.1
*.default.svc.cluster.local has address 10.4.2.8
*.default.svc.cluster.local has address 10.4.2.6
*.default.svc.cluster.local has address 10.4.8.6
*.default.svc.cluster.local has address 10.4.17.4
*.default.svc.cluster.local has address 10.7.240.9
```

It's pretty difficult to determine what this means—if there is more than one service in the namespace, it's really not useful. Similarly, you can use a wildcard for the namespace label, or even both. But it's difficult to find much meaning in the responses.

There are some use cases that make more sense. For example, you can use this to query for all of the endpoints of a service, as shown in Example 6-25.

Example 6-25. Wildcard queries for endpoints

```
dnstools# host kube-dns.kube-system.svc.cluster.local.
kube-dns.kube-system.svc.cluster.local has address 10.7.240.10
dnstools#
dnstools# host *.kube-dns.kube-system.svc.cluster.local.
*.kube-dns.kube-system.svc.cluster.local has address 10.4.17.6
*.kube-dns.kube-system.svc.cluster.local has address 10.4.8.7
```

In this example, the first query shows that kube-dns is a clusterIP service. However, if we query for the endpoints using *.<service>.<namespace>.svc.cluster.local, CoreDNS will return the two endpoint records. This is the only way to get this information via DNS: the SRV queries usually used for this work only for headless services.

This behavior is certainly not according to the Kubernetes DNS specification, but it can be useful in some cases nonetheless. The valid places to use a wildcard are for the endpoint, service name, and namespace in an A record request, and those same labels plus the port and protocol in an SRV record request. You can use wildcards for multiple labels, as well.

Autopath and the Dreaded ndots:5

One of the common challenges with DNS in Kubernetes is the way in which *resolv.conf* for pods is configured. To allow using short names for services—service instead of service.namespace.svc.cluster.local—the kubelet sets the search path in a pod's *resolv.conf* to the following domains, in the order shown:

1. <namespace>.svc.cluster.local: allows names like <service>
2. svc.cluster.local: allows names like <service>.<namespace>
3. cluster.local: allows names like <service>.<namespace>.svc
4. The host search path, which is usually a couple of domains

The first domain works really well when you are resolving in-cluster names. You can just request a service by name, and it will find the one in your local namespace. It allows configurations to remain unchanged when deploying an application into a different namespace. Similarly, the second and third allow the names to remain the same when moving between clusters.

However, when resolving an external name, we run into trouble. For the search path to work properly, kubelet also sets the ndots option to five. That means that any domain name with fewer than five dots is considered to be a possible relative domain, and so the search path will be applied. Example 6-26 shows the result.

Example 6-26. Querying an external name with ndots:5

```
dnstools# host -v example.com
Trying "example.com.default.svc.cluster.local"
Trying "example.com.svc.cluster.local"
Trying "example.com.cluster.local"
Trying "example.com.c.belamaric-com.internal"
Trying "example.com.google.internal"
Trying "example.com"
;; ->>HEADER<<- opcode: QUERY, status: NOERROR, id: 11173
;; flags: qr rd ra; QUERY: 1, ANSWER: 1, AUTHORITY: 0, ADDITIONAL: 0
...snipped...
```

This means to resolve the single query, *five failed queries* were made before the final successful sixth query. Each one of these was initiated by the client, sent over the network, processed, and responded to by CoreDNS. If your workloads make a lot of lookups of external names, this can dramatically increase the load on CoreDNS.

A number of solutions are available. One is to use the dnsConfig field of the PodSpec to set your own, custom policy. That works, but it requires everyone who is using the cluster to configure their own pod DNS if they use a lot of external names. Relying on users to remember to do this is not likely to be effective. Similarly, we could ask users to always use fully qualified domain names (FQDNs), including the trailing ., but that seems like an unlikely fantasy.

Another solution is an upcoming node local cache, which is Beta in Kubernetes 1.15 and should be GA in 1.16 or 1.17. This places a special, small caching-only build of CoreDNS on every node in the cluster. It forwards anything not in the cache to the central CoreDNS service over Transmission Control Protocol (TCP), which is more reliable than UDP and avoids possible 5-second timeouts. This is a pretty good solution,[10] but it is only in alpha as of Kubernetes 1.14, so it will be a while before it is available everywhere. Additionally, it uses a small amount of extra resources on every node, and each node's local cache is not highly available (only a single instance runs).

CoreDNS has another solution, called autopath. Using this plug-in, CoreDNS will figure out the search path on the server side. When it recognizes a query that looks like it is the first in a search (e.g., example.com.default.svc.cluster.local), it will iterate over that search path itself, internally. This is much, much faster because there is no network involved; it's just an internal loop. If it gets a result, it will return a CNAME pointing to that result, as shown in Example 6-27.

---

10 It also allows setting your stub domains (forwarders) up on each node, further reducing strain on the central DNS, and fixes an issue with DNS queries filling up the Linux conntrack table.

Example 6-27. An autopath response

```
dnstools# dig example.com +search

; <<>> DiG 9.11.3 <<>> example.com +search
;; global options: +cmd
;; Got answer:
;; WARNING: .local is reserved for Multicast DNS
;; You are currently testing what happens when an mDNS query is leaked to DNS
;; ->>HEADER<<- opcode: QUERY, status: NOERROR, id: 3370
;; flags: qr rd ra; QUERY: 1, ANSWER: 2, AUTHORITY: 0, ADDITIONAL: 1

;; OPT PSEUDOSECTION:
; EDNS: version: 0, flags:; udp: 4096
;; QUESTION SECTION:
;example.com.default.svc.cluster.local. IN A

;; ANSWER SECTION:
example.com.default.svc.cluster.local. 30 IN CNAME example.com.
example.com.            30      IN      A       93.184.216.34

;; Query time: 9 msec
;; SERVER: 10.7.240.9#53(10.7.240.9)
;; WHEN: Tue Apr 02 01:29:42 UTC 2019
;; MSG SIZE  rcvd: 155
```

The biggest downside to using autopath is scalability. To figure out the search path, CoreDNS needs to know the namespace of the client pod. The only information it has on the client pod is the source IP address of the query, so CoreDNS needs to use that to figure out the namespace of the client. Enabling pods verified mode does this, but it increases the memory consumption as described in "Pod Options" on page 111.

Zone Transfer Support

CoreDNS supports zone transfers (AXFR) of the kubernetes zone. This is a wonderful debugging tool because it allows you to see all the records available for your Kubernetes cluster with a single request. If you have pod IPs that are routable in your organization, it can also provide direct access to headless service endpoints by external clients.

To enable zone transfers, you must configure the transfer to option in the kubernetes plug-in. This works in the same manner as other plug-ins, as described in "transfer to" on page 51. An example is shown in Example 6-28.

Example 6-28. Configuring zone transfers

```
kubernetes cluster.local in-addr.arpa ip6.arpa {
  pods verified
  upstream
  fallthrough in-addr.arpa ip6.arpa
  transfer to *
}
```

To try a zone transfer, use `host -t axfr cluster.local.`, as in Example 6-29.

Example 6-29. Zone transfer of cluster.local

```
dnstools# host -t axfr cluster.local. coredns
Trying "cluster.local"

;; ->>HEADER<<- opcode: QUERY, status: NOERROR, id: 64392
;; flags: qr aa; QUERY: 1, ANSWER: 24, AUTHORITY: 0, ADDITIONAL: 0

;; QUESTION SECTION:
;cluster.local.                  IN      AXFR

;; ANSWER SECTION:
cluster.local.          5       IN      SOA     ns.dns.cluster.local. hostmaster...
...snipped...
kubernetes-dashboard.kube-system.svc.cluster.local. 5 IN SRV 0 100 443 kubernetes...
default-http-backend.kube-system.svc.cluster.local. 5 IN A 10.7.242.43
default-http-backend.kube-system.svc.cluster.local. 5 IN SRV 0 100 80 default-http...

Received 482 bytes from 10.7.240.9#53 in 5 ms
```

IXFR is not supported, and deprecated pod records are not transferred. Also, if you are using `fallthrough`, records in *cluster.local* that are served by another plug-in will not be transferred. Due to a bug with a missing NS record, the zone transfer is also not currently compatible with BIND. This means that although the zone transfer can be useful in some limited cases as described, it still needs some work to fully integrate with traditional DNS infastructure.

Exposing Services Externally

The Kubernetes DNS specification covers headless and `clusterIP` services. Those types of services allow access from inside the cluster. But often we want a service that is running in the cluster to be accessible throughout the organization. How do we allow clients external to the cluster to reach a service? Kubernetes provides several answers to that question: External IPs, NodePort services, LoadBalancer services, and Ingress resources.

These methods allow traffic that reaches the external IP address to be directed to the service. But how can the clients *discover* those IP addresses? Kubernetes does not provide a standard answer here, in that the typical shipping components in a Kubernetes distribution cannot provide this service discovery.

One solution is to use the external DNS Kubernetes incubator project (*https://oreil.ly/ 7nGIW*). This project provides an optional controller that interacts with a DNS server to add records for these external IPs and Ingresses. This assumes that the external DNS server that controls the domain for that service can be modified via an API. The external DNS project supports more than a dozen different DNS services, including Google Cloud DNS, AWS Route53, Infoblox, and CoreDNS running with etcd and the etcd plug-in.

If your needs are simpler than those provided by the external DNS project, you can also expose your LoadBalancer and External IP services using a special CoreDNS plug-in called k8s_external. This allows you to specify a zone to publish the external IP addresses on, in the form <service>.<namespace>.<zone>. Example 6-30 shows an example configuration.

Example 6-30. Configuring an external zone

```
k8s_external services.example.com {
  apex services
}
```

This plug-in works only if the kubernetes plug-in is also configured. It will handle the SOA and NS records for the apex, allowing delegation to CoreDNS for that zone. The k8s_external plug-in also offers a ttl option to allow control of the TTL for these records.

Using a Second CoreDNS

Rather than exposing your internal cluster DNS to external users, you should consider running a second deployment of CoreDNS just for external names. This protects your cluster DNS from denial-of-service attacks from outside the cluster. Losing your cluster DNS will usually take down a lot of services in your cluster, so use a little extra resources to avoid some heartburn.

Modifying the Available Records

There are several ways in which you can tweak the configuration of the kubernetes plug-in to tailor the way records are presented to handle special use cases. For example, in a multitenant use case, you might want to run a separate CoreDNS that makes records for only certain namespaces available. Or, you might want to make endpoint names more predictable, if you need to feed those names into a process that cannot look them up easily. Using these configuration options can veer outside the standard Kubernetes DNS specification, so you should use them with caution.

Recall the discussion about endpoint records from "Kubernetes DNS Specification" on page 82. There, we describe how CoreDNS decided on the name for an endpoint A record in an SRV response. By default, CoreDNS will use the "dashed" version of the IP address of the pod as the label for the pod. This means that you cannot know the endpoint name ahead of time, and it also means that the hostname in the pod does not match the label in DNS.

The `endpoint_pod_names` option alleviates this problem. It still allows customization of the hostname and subdomain, but if the hostname is not set in the PodSpec, CoreDNS will use the name of the pod, instead of the dashed form of the IP address. Technically, this is still within the DNS specification, but relying on it is not.

Another way to modify how endpoints are handled is to enable the `ignore empty_service` option. This will reply with NXDOMAIN instead of a success response with no data. You can use this in combination with host search path modifications to direct traffic to a different cluster. That is, sending NXDOMAIN means that the client will continue with the next entry in the search path, which could be configured to point to a secondary cluster.

If you don't use headless services, you might want to save the resources associated with loading Endpoints resources. You can disable the Endpoints watch by using the `nodendpoints` option. Queries to headless services and to endpoints will return NXDOMAIN.

For special-purpose use cases, such as multitenancy, it is possible to limit the scope of records made available to the user. You can do this by using the `namespaces` or `labels` options.

The `namespaces` option accepts a list of namespaces; only records in those namespaces will be loaded and served. If you dedicate specific nodes and namespaces to a tenant, you can modify the options to the kubelet to set the name server selected to a CoreDNS service. This CoreDNS would be configured to only return records for that tenant's namespaces.

The `labels` option works in the same manner, but you provide a label selector instead of a list of namespaces.

The integration with Kubernetes is one of the most common use cases for CoreDNS. This chapter covered that integration in detail. You learned about the basics of Kubernetes internals, and how CoreDNS is configured, deployed, and operated within Kubernetes. We also covered customizations and alternate ways to use these two products together.

In previous chapters, you also learned about other plug-ins for CoreDNS that pulled data from other sources as well as Kubernetes, for both service discovery and traditional DNS. But the power of CoreDNS does not just come from its ability to use multiple backend data sources. It also offers the ability to modify DNS requests and responses as they flow through. Chapter 7 focuses on those capabilities.

Manipulating Queries and Responses

CoreDNS gives you a great deal of control over what happens to a request as it goes through the plug-in chain, and what response is provided to the client. This allows you to tailor the DNS behavior to your particular environment and use cases. For example, you can easily generate standard names within specific zones using the `template` plug-in, and you can transparently redirect traffic using the `rewrite` plug-in.

This chapter discusses a few of the most commonly used plug-ins for manipulating requests and responses in this way.

The template Plug-in

The `template` plug-in allows you to fabricate answers based solely upon the request. A common use case for this is the creation of answers to PTR queries, without having to actually write them all out in a zone file, as shown in Example 7-1.[1]

Example 7-1. Answering PTR queries with template

```
example.com:5300 in-addr.arpa:5300 {
    # Match host-a-b-c-d.example.com A requests and return a.b.c.d
    template IN A example.com {
      match (^|[.])host-(?P<a>[0-9]*)-(?P<b>[0-9]*)-(?P<c>[0-9]*)-(?P<d>[0-9]*)↵
      [.]example[.]com[.]$
      answer "{{ .Name }} 60 IN A {{ .Group.a }}.{{ .Group.b }}.{{ .Group.c }}.↵
      {{ .Group.d }}"
      fallthrough
    }
```

---

1 The ↵ indicates the line has been wrapped here, but should not be in the actual Corefile.

```
# Match d.c.b.a.in-addr.arpa PTR requests and return host-a-b-c-d.example.com
template IN PTR in-addr.arpa {
  match ^(?P<d>[0-9]*)[.](?P<c>[0-9]*)[.](?P<b>[0-9]*)[.](?P<a>[0-9]*)↵
  [.]in-addr[.]arpa[.]$
  answer "{{ .Name }} 60 IN PTR host-{{ .Group.a }}-{{ .Group.b }}↵
  -{{ .Group.c }}-{{ .Group.d }}.example.com."
}

forward . /etc/resolv.conf
}
```

The `fallthrough` option in this example allows queries that do not match these patterns to be served by subsequent plug-ins—`forward` in this case, but you could also use *file*, which comes after *template* in the plug-in list. Example 7-2 shows the results of queries to this instance of CoreDNS.

Example 7-2. Querying with the template plug-in

```
$ dig +nostats +nocmd +nocomments -p 5300 -t ptr 1.2.3.4.in-addr.arpa @localhost
;1.2.3.4.in-addr.arpa.          IN      PTR
1.2.3.4.in-addr.arpa.   60      IN      PTR     host-4-3-2-1.example.com.
$ dig +nostats +nocmd +nocomments -p 5300 host-1-2-3-4.example.com @localhost
;host-1-2-3-4.example.com.      IN      A
host-1-2-3-4.example.com. 60    IN      A       1.2.3.4
```

Example 7-3 presents the general syntax of `template`.

Example 7-3. Template syntax

```
template CLASS TYPE [ZONE...] {
    match REGEX...
    answer RR
    additional RR
    authority RR
    rcode CODE
    upstream
    fallthrough [ZONE...]
}
```

The top-line arguments of CLASS TYPE and ZONE(s) are used to match the incoming request. Next, the regular expression defined in `match` is checked; if it does not meet the criteria, the query will just be passed on. The `answer`, `additional`, `authority`, and `rcode` options correspond to the response. Internally, the `template` plug-in uses the Go text/template library, so the RR values must be in Go template format, which is described at *https://golang.org/pkg/text/template*.

Note that because of how environment variables are handled in the *Corefile*, when using a Go template variable, you must use an expression like {{ $variable }} instead of {{$variable}}. These are equivalent in the Go template, but the latter will result in an environment variable substitution in the *Corefile*, as described in "Environment Variables" on page 34.

You can also use this plug-in to block names that you do not want queried. The *Corefile* in Example 7-4 will answer NXDOMAIN for any request for the *example.com* domain.[2]

Example 7-4. Template to return NXDOMAIN for example.com

```
.:5300 {
    template IN ANY example.com {
      rcode NXDOMAIN
    }
    forward . /etc/resolv.conf
}
```

When we try to query a domain name in *example.com*, we get an NXDOMAIN response, as demonstrated in Example 7-5.

Example 7-5. An NXDOMAIN response from the template plug-in

```
$ dig +nostats +nocmd -p 5300 www.example.com @localhost
;; Got answer:
;; ->>HEADER<<- opcode: QUERY, status: NXDOMAIN, id: 37133
;; flags: qr aa rd; QUERY: 1, ANSWER: 0, AUTHORITY: 0, ADDITIONAL: 1
;; WARNING: recursion requested but not available

;; OPT PSEUDOSECTION:
; EDNS: version: 0, flags:; udp: 4096
;; QUESTION SECTION:
;www.example.com.              IN      A
```

The template plug-in is used to generate records based on the request. Another feature that CoreDNS provides is the ability to modify the request and response. The rewrite plug-in, described next, makes that possible.

---

2 In this context, ANY matches all query types, including A, PTR, and so on, not just the query type ANY.

The rewrite Plug-in

One of the earliest plug-ins built for CoreDNS was the `rewrite` plug-in. It was originally based on the `HTTP` plug-in of the same name in Caddy. The purpose of this plug-in is to modify the request and/or the response. For requests, the queried record type, name, class, or EDNS0 options can be modified. For responses, the time-to-live (TTL) and in some cases the domain names of records in the answer section can be rewritten. The basic syntax for this plug-in is shown in Example 7-6.

Example 7-6. Rewrite basic syntax

```
rewrite [continue|stop] FIELD [FROM TO|FROM TTL]  [ answer name FROM TO ]
```

The details of each option are as follows:

`continue` *and* `stop`
> Determine how multiple rules are handled, as described in "Multiple rewrite Rules" on page 128.

`FIELD`
> Defines what component of the request you want to modify. Valid values are `type`, `class`, `name`, `edns0`, or `ttl`.

`FROM`
> Defines the predicate for the rewrite. That is, fields are not rewritten unconditionally; rather they are rewritten only if they match the `FROM` criteria. For `class` and `type`, this is simply the current class or type in the query. For `name` and `ttl`, it is a bit more complicated. It can be one of the qualifiers `exact`, `suffix`, `prefix`, `substring`, or `regex`, along with the name match expression. If not specified, `exact` will be used for matching.

`TO` *or* `TTL`
> Specify the value to which to set the field.

`answer name FROM TO`
> Can optionally be used with name rules to rewrite the answer section.

Why would you want to rewrite the request or response in this way? One of the most common reasons is to enable the use of the same Transport Layer Security (TLS) certificate even when using different names to access a site; for example, from inside a Kubernetes cluster and from outside the cluster. This works like a canonical name (CNAME) record but is transparent to the client.

Consider a site name *api.example.com* that is running in a Kubernetes cluster. Because the TLS certificate for the site is for *api.example.com*, any client trying to

---

access the site must use that name to reach the site, or it will not be able to verify the authenticity of the site. However, when accessing the site from inside the cluster, we would rather not have the request go to *api.example.com*, because that will cause traffic to hairpin: it will exit the cluster, go back through the cloud load balancer, and finally come back through the Kubernetes NodePort, where it likely will have yet another hop to get to a pod that services the request. This all adds a lot of latency. Instead, we would prefer to be able to access the site by its cluster DNS name, such as *api.example.svc.cluster.local*.

One option would be to add that name to the TLS certificate. However, this could be running in many different clusters, divided by environment (development, test, staging, or production), or by region, and each of these clusters might have a different cluster domain. We would need to add it for every different cluster domain name. Instead, `rewrite` can make this simple. Example 7-7 shows a *Corefile* that handles this scenario by using a `rewrite` rule that modifies the Question section of the query to look for *api.example.svc.cluster.local* if it matches *api.example.com*.

Example 7-7. Rewriting the query name

```
.:53 {
  errors
  health
  rewrite name api.example.com. api.example.svc.cluster.local.
  kubernetes cluster.local in-addr.arpa ip6.arpa {
    fallthrough in-addr.arpa ip6.arpa
  }
  prometheus :9153
  forward . /etc/resolv.conf
  cache 30
  loop
  reload
  loadbalance
}
```

Example 7-8 shows what happens when we query for these records.

Example 7-8. Querying with rewrite

```
dnstools# host api.example.svc.cluster.local
api.example.svc.cluster.local has address 10.7.249.102
dnstools# host api.example.com
api.example.com has address 10.7.249.102
```

Suppose that we have many different services, not just `api`, that we want to have the same behavior. The `rewrite` plug-in offers a regular expression matching rule for names to make this possible; we use the rewrite rule `rewrite name regex ^([^\.]*)`

`\.example\.com\.$ {1}.example.svc.cluster.local.` instead of `rewrite name api.example.com api.example.svc.cluster.local.` Example 7-9 shows how the queries work with this rule in place.

Example 7-9. Query with regular expression rewrite

```
dnstools# host api.example.com
api.example.svc.cluster.local has address 10.7.249.102
dnstools# host foo.example.com
foo.example.svc.cluster.local has address 10.7.251.161
```

If you look closely, you will see a problem. The query is for *api.example.com*, but what comes back is *api.example.svc.cluster.local*. With this rule in place, the response returned by the server has a different domain name in the Question section than that sent by the client originally. For security reasons, some DNS resolver libraries will reject a response from a server if the Question section of the response does not match the Question section of the request that the library sent. With this configuration, many clients will reject the response.

With the previous exact match rule, the `rewrite` plug-in automatically filled in the original question. For the regular expression rules, it does not do this automatically, and so we must use the `answer name` option of the `rewrite` plug-in, as shown in Example 7-10.

Example 7-10. Rewrite rule with answer name

```
rewrite {
  name regex ^([^\.]*)\.example\.com\.$ {1}.example.svc.cluster.local.
  answer name ^([^\.]*)\.example\.svc\.cluster\.local\.$ {1}.example.com.
}
```

Trying the queries again in Example 7-11, we now see that the question and answer names match.

Example 7-11. Query with regular expression and answer rule

```
dnstools# host api.example.com
api.example.com has address 10.7.249.102
dnstools# host foo.example.com
foo.example.com has address 10.7.251.161
dnstools# host bar.example.com
Host bar.example.com not found: 3(NXDOMAIN)
```

The last query, for *bar.example.com*, translates into *bar.example.svc.cluster.local*, which is a nonexistent service, thus resulting in the NXDOMAIN just as if the user had entered *bar.example.svc.cluster.local* directly.

Rewriting the name is one feature of this plug-in. But it's also possible to modify the request in other ways. The next section describes how to use the `rewrite` plug-in to modify the EDNS0 options for the request.

Using the rewrite Plug-in for EDNS0 Options

RFC 6891 defines "Extension Mechanisms for DNS (EDNS(0))," which allows additional options to be included in DNS requests and responses. Another powerful use of the `rewrite` plug-in is to manipulate these EDNS0 options in the request.

The `rewrite` plug-in allows you to add and remove options with this syntax:

Example 7-12. EDNS0 rewrite syntax

```
rewrite [continue|stop] edns0 TYPE [set|replace|append] TYPE-FIELDS
```

TYPE here defines the EDNS0 type to rewrite. As of CoreDNS 1.5.0, the supported values for TYPE are `local`, `nsid`, and `subnet`. TYPE-FIELDS vary based on what the TYPE is.

The `set` action will set the option to the specified value, either creating a new option or overwriting an existing option in the request. The `replace` action is similar, but will not create a new option: it will modify the option only if it already exists. Matching for both `set` and `replace` is based on the EDNS0 option code. The `append` action will always add the option, even if it already exists. This is useful for options that can be repeated.

The EDNS0 rewrites are especially useful for "edge" deployments of CoreDNS. These are deployments in a home or branch office that provide DNS to local devices. By using the `rewrite` plug-in with EDNS0 rules, upstream name servers can receive information about the deployment location and modify their responses, as needed.

For example, the `subnet` type allows you to set the EDNS Client Subnet (ECS) option. Upstream DNS servers can use this option to provide different responses to clients on different subnets, as described in RFC 7871. The rule `rewrite edns0 subnet set 24 64` will use the first 24 bits or 64 bits of the client's IPv4 or IPv6 source IP address, respectively, for the value of the ECS option. This informs the upstream DNS server what subnet the client is on so that it can customize the response.

The `local` EDNS0 type offers the ability to perform the same sort of thing but using additional information that might be specific to your use case. For example, Infoblox uses this to identify the customer and even user of the client making a query, and apply organizational policy to the request, which we describe in detail in "Case Study: Infoblox's BloxOne Threat Defense" on page 137. The `local` type takes two TYPE-FIELDs, `option code` and `data`. The data can be a simple string, or it can be a hexadecimal string, which will be packed into the option data as binary data. In fact, the data may be a variable, using any of these fields:

{qname}
> The question name.

{qtype}
> The question type.

{client_ip}
> The client's source IP address.

{client_port}
> The client's source port.

{protocol}
> The protocol used for the request.

{server_ip}
> The server's IP address on which the request was received.

{server_port}
> The server's port on which the request was received.

Example 7-13 shows some samples. If the metadata plug-in is enabled, you can also use any metadata value. "The metadata Plug-in" on page 129 discusses metadata in more detail.

Example 7-13. EDNS0 local rewrites

```
rewrite edns0 local set 0xffaa some-value
rewrite edns0 local set 0xffab 0xaabbccdd
rewrite edns0 local set 0xffac {client_ip}
rewrite edns0 local set 0xffad {protocol}
```

The examples so far all stop after the first rewrite is applied. The next section explains how to perform multiple rewrites on the same request.

Multiple rewrite Rules

As mentioned in the syntax description, it is possible to specify multiple rewrite rules. By default, the first matching rule will be applied and rule processing will stop. To enable multiple rules to affect the same query, you can specify the continue option, as shown in Example 7-14. This example will allow the ChaosNet class query for a TXT record attached to bind.version to return the Kubernetes DNS version TXT record instead.

Example 7-14. Allowing multiple rules

```
rewrite continue class CH IN
rewrite stop name bind.version dns-version.cluster.local
```

When a query matches the first rule, the `rewrite` will be applied, and the processing will continue with the next rule. Example 7-15 shows how CoreDNS responds to a few different queries with this configuration.

Example 7-15. Query with multiple rules

```
dnstools# host -t txt dns-version.cluster.local.
dns-version.cluster.local descriptive text "1.0.1"
dnstools# host -t txt bind.version.
bind.version descriptive text "1.0.1"
dnstools# host -t txt -c ch bind.version.
;; Warning: Message parser reports malformed message packet.
bind.version descriptive text "1.0.1"
```

The last query in the example shows a warning about a malformed packet. This is because the answer class does not match the question class. Unfortunately, CoreDNS does not offer an equivalent of the `answer name` option for class rewrites.

Note that when multiple rewrite rules are specified within a server block, they are processed in order. It also does not matter whether other plug-in directives appear between the rewrite rules; they will still be processed one after another, in the order listed. You can find more examples of the `rewrite` plug-in at *https://coredns.io/ plugins/rewrite*.

The `rewrite` plug-in can also work in concert with another plug-in, the `metadata` plug-in, to extract and enhance the request in different ways. We describe this plug-in in the next section.

The metadata Plug-in

The `metadata` plug-in is an interesting one. It does not manipulate the request or response itself. However, it enables other plug-ins to make data about the request available to be used in manipulations.

Any plug-in can be a metadata provider or consumer (or both). When enabled, each plug-in in the chain gets a "sneak peek" at the request. It can then calculate (or look up) metadata based on the request and "publish" it for use by other plug-ins. The plug-ins that use the data are the consumers.

As of CoreDNS 1.5.0, there are two in-tree consumers, `log` and `rewrite`, and no in-tree providers.[3] Future versions will enable `trace`, `template`, and perhaps `dnstap` as in-tree consumers, and `kubernetes` as an in-tree producer. The out-of-tree producer `metadata_edns0` might also move in-tree.

Let's look at the *metadata_edns0* producer, an example configuration shown in Example 7-16. This is in the CoreDNS GitHub organization (i.e, under *https://github.com/coredns*), but is an external plug-in; it is neither in the *coredns* repository itself nor is it compiled in by default. It provides the reverse of the `rewrite edns0` function. That is, it will unpack an EDNS0 option into a metadata value, allowing it to be logged or reused in a different rewrite.

Example 7-16. Unpacking EDNS0 data into metadata

```
metadata_edns0 {
    client_id 0xffed address
    group_id 0xffee hex 16
}
```

This configuration will read the EDNS0 local option `0xffed` as if it were an IP address and publish it under the metadata name `{/metadata_edns0/client_id}`. Similarly, it will unpack 16 bytes of option `0xffee`, encode it as hexadecimal, and make it available under the metadata name `{/metadata_edns0/group_id}`.

A simple use case for this, using only in-tree plug-ins and the `metadata_edns0` plug-in, would be to add a "site" EDNS0 option in the edge deployment of CoreDNS, and then decode that in the upstream CoreDNS server and log it, allowing easy determination of the sites from which queries are coming.

The `firewall` plug-in is an out-of-tree plug-in in development that allows blocking of DNS requests. This plug-in will also be a metadata consumer, allowing blocking of requests based on metadata. Combined with publishing data from the `kubernetes` plug-in, you can use this to implement multitenant service discovery in Kubernetes.

There are many powerful use cases that can be addressed because all of the plug-ins support the `metadata` functionality.

Signing Responses with the DNS Security Extensions

The DNS Security Extensions (DNSSEC) allow the administrators of DNS zones to cryptographically "sign" the records in those zones as well as allow the administrators of recursive DNS servers to configure those servers to cryptographically validate

---

3 CoreDNS 1.5.1 adds metadata publishing to the kubernetes plugin.

signed records. This provides protection against poisoning the cache of the recursive DNS servers—inducing them to cache bogus records from the signed zones, as might otherwise be possible using the Kaminsky attack (*https://oreil.ly/llaq0*), for example.

DNSSEC is fairly complex and is documented in about a dozen RFCs. The core RFCs alone, RFCs 4033, 4034, and 4035, are more than 100 pages. We won't take the time to explain DNSSEC theory here, but if you're interested, see the discussion in the book *DNS and BIND* (O'Reilly), in particular the *Security* chapter.

Mercifully, CoreDNS aims to make DNSSEC simple to set up and simple to administer. It doesn't support all of the DNSSEC functionality that BIND does, but you might well not need all of the bells and whistles.

Managing a DNSSEC-Signed Primary Zone

If you run CoreDNS as a primary DNS server, using the `auto` or `file` plug-in, you need to sign the zone data file yourself. The tools for signing zone data files aren't included as part of CoreDNS, but there are several good open source packages that will let you generate keys, sign zones, and then manage those signed zones (e.g., re-signing them and rolling keys over), including BIND 9 and OpenDNSSEC. In our examples, we use two tools from the BIND 9 distribution: `dnssec-keygen` and `dnssec-signzone`.

Let's begin with this simple zone data file for the zone *foo.example*, called *db.foo.example*, as shown in Example 7-17.

Example 7-17. foo.example zone data file, before signing

```
@       IN  SOA ns1.foo.example. root.foo.example. (
        2019041900
        3600
        600
        604800
        600 )

        IN  NS  ns1.foo.example.
        IN  NS  ns2.foo.example.

ns1     IN  A   10.0.0.53
        IN  AAAA  2001:db8:42:1::53

ns2     IN  A   10.0.1.53
        IN  AAAA  2001:db8:42:2::53

www     IN  A   10.0.0.1
        IN  AAAA  2001:db8:42:1::1
```

First, we generate a DNSSEC key pair for the zone with `dnssec-keygen`. In Example 7-18, we specify the type of key, ECDSAP256SHA256 (Elliptic Curve P-256 with SHA-256; a good choice for generating small signatures), as well as the domain name of the zone, *foo.example*.[4]

Example 7-18. Using dnssec-keygen to generate a key pair

```
% dnssec-keygen -a ECDSAP256SHA256 foo.example
Generating key pair.
Kfoo.example.+013+50136
```

This first run generates what's known as the Zone-Signing Key (ZSK) pair. The private key of this key pair will be used to sign all of the records in the zone, and the public key will be used to validate all of the records in the zone.

Now, we run `dnssec-keygen` again with a new argument, `-f KSK`, to generate a Key-Signing Key (KSK) pair, for *foo.example*, as shown in Example 7-19.

Example 7-19. Using dnssec-keygen to generate a KSK pair

```
dnssec-keygen -a ECDSAP256SHA256 -f KSK foo.example
Generating key pair.
Kfoo.example.+013+12016
```

As the name suggests, the private key of the KSK pair is used only to sign the keys in the zone. The reason we usually use two key pairs in DNSSEC is because keys used frequently to sign a lot of records (like the ZSK) need to be "rolled over" on a regular basis, but our parent zone needs to include information about our keys in their zone, too. It would be a hassle to let our parent zone know each time we rolled over our ZSK. So we introduce another key pair, the KSK, which is used only to sign keys (hence, less data) and therefore doesn't need to be rolled over as frequently. Those are the keys our parent zone knows about.

---

4 There are other algorithms that you can use for signing zones, of course. RSA with SHA-256, SHA-384, or SHA-512 is a good choice for compatibility with most DNS server implementations that perform DNSSEC validation, though it does generate longer signatures. Note that CoreDNS doesn't support NSEC3, so don't choose that option.

A Note on Key Rollovers

There's a lot more to key rollovers than we have space to cover here. The U National Institutes of Standards and Technology (NIST) recommend, in its *Secure Domain Name System (DNS) Deployment Guide* establishing a KSK rollover interval of between 1 and 2 years, and a ZSK rollover interval of between 1 and 3 months. For much more discussion of key rollovers, see that guide, also called *NIST Special Publication 800-81-2*, as well as RFC 4641, *DNSSEC Operational Practices*.

Next, we extract the DNSKEY records for both the ZSK and KSK pairs from the appropriate files and add them to the zone data file for *foo.example*. The keys are in the files *Kfoo.example.+013+50136.key* and *Kfoo.example.+013+12016.key*, whose filenames are just the basenames printed by dnssec-keygen with ".key" appended. Example 7-20 presents the results.

Example 7-20. foo.example zone data file with DNSKEY records added

```
@        IN  SOA  ns1.foo.example. root.foo.example. (
         2019041900
         3600
         600
         604800
         600 )

         IN  NS  ns1.foo.example.
         IN  NS  ns2.foo.example.

foo.example. IN DNSKEY 256 3 13 QJwZJ7i/25fRhGM0RwnefZD6FOAlFiyjK8+RkBKBA9tUzn4t+...
foo.example. IN DNSKEY 257 3 13 JVbwBdbQodjT+bOXkYxLVh8cpnHeK3mIpdMQ0llQnYWWB7Ps0...

ns1      IN  A  10.0.0.53
         IN  AAAA  2001:db8:42:1::53

ns2      IN  A  10.0.1.53
         IN  AAAA  2001:db8:42:2::53

www      IN  A  10.0.0.1
         IN  AAAA  2001:db8:42:1::1
```

Now, finally, we can sign the zone using dnssec-signzone, as illustrated in Example 7-21.

Example 7-21. Signing the zone with dnssec-signzone

```
% dnssec-signzone -o foo.example db.foo.example
dnssec-signzone: warning: db.foo.example:10: using RFC1035 TTL semantics
Verifying the zone using the following algorithms: ECDSAP256SHA256.
Zone fully signed:
Algorithm: ECDSAP256SHA256: KSKs: 1 active, 0 stand-by, 0 revoked
                            ZSKs: 1 active, 0 stand-by, 0 revoked
db.foo.example.signed
```

The result is a zone data file that includes the original records plus the two DNSKEY records and signatures, in the form of RRSIG records. It's much longer than the previous, so we'll just show you the beginning in Example 7-22 so that you know we're telling the truth.

Example 7-22. The signed foo.example zone

```
; File written on Mon Jun  3 14:39:29 2019
; dnssec_signzone version 9.10.3
foo.example.             3600     IN SOA  ns1.foo.example. root.foo.example. (
                                          2019041900 ; serial
                                          3600       ; refresh (1 hour)
                                          600        ; retry (10 minutes)
                                          604800     ; expire (1 week)
                                          600        ; minimum (10 minutes)
                                          )
                         3600     RRSIG   SOA 13 2 3600 (
                                          20190703203929 20190603203929 50136
                                          foo.example.
                                          ZTfVklyEsBXffy7ucbBmAe8AoOoTXk0rRmJZ
                                          y9/FZPTELVuT2O2FwnAJPgU//HoOdsSaD21u
                                          EVaKhV6QPhVy7Q== )
                         3600     NS      ns1.foo.example.
                         3600     NS      ns2.foo.example.
                         3600     RRSIG   NS 13 2 3600 (
                                          20190703203929 20190603203929 50136
                                          foo.example.
                                          iRpaN03PK/pNb03m28PAHVOv4KughmtpNw30
                                          H3OpdM3h7P0/Ka0Z86j7FQS2UC6p79/ap2I+
                                          18ZzgsEHEbzxLg== )
```

All CoreDNS requires is that we instruct it to load the new, signed zone data file, as shown in Example 7-23.

Example 7-23. Corefile loading a signed zone data file

```
foo.example {
    file db.foo.example.signed
    errors
    log
}
```

This will return the signatures and other DNSSEC records to queriers that set the DNSSEC OK bit in their queries, as demonstrated in Example 7-24.

Example 7-24. Hello World in Python

```
% dig soa foo.example. +dnssec +norec

; <<>> DiG 9.10.3 <<>> soa foo.example. +dnssec +norec
; (1 server found)
;; global options: +cmd
;; Got answer:
;; ->>HEADER<<- opcode: QUERY, status: NOERROR, id: 279
;; flags: qr aa; QUERY: 1, ANSWER: 2, AUTHORITY: 3, ADDITIONAL: 1

;; OPT PSEUDOSECTION:
; EDNS: version: 0, flags: do; udp: 4096
;; QUESTION SECTION:
;foo.example.            IN      SOA

;; ANSWER SECTION:
foo.example.        3600    IN      SOA     ns1.foo.example. root.foo.example.
 2019041900 3600 600 604800 600
foo.example.        3600    IN      RRSIG     SOA 13 2 3600 20190703203929
 20190603203929 50136 foo.example.
 ZTfVklyEsBXffy7ucbBmAe8AoOoTXk0rRmJZy9/FZPTELVuT2O2FwnAJ
 PgU//HoOdsSaD21uEVaKhV6QPhVy7Q==

;; AUTHORITY SECTION:
foo.example.        3600    IN      NS      ns1.foo.example.
foo.example.        3600    IN      NS      ns2.foo.example.
foo.example.        3600    IN      RRSIG     NS 13 2 3600 20190703203929
 20190603203929 50136 foo.example.
 iRpaN03PK/pNb03m28PAHVOv4KughmtpNw30H3OpdM3h7P0/Ka0Z86j7
 FQS2UC6p79/ap2I+18ZzgsEHEbzxLg==

;; Query time: 0 msec
;; SERVER: 127.0.0.1#53(127.0.0.1)
;; WHEN: Mon Jun 03 14:50:47 PDT 2019
;; MSG SIZE  rcvd: 434
```

The rest of maintaining a DNSSEC-signed zone—resigning the zone before signatures expire, rolling keys over—is up to you. Unfortunately, CoreDNS provides no help there. But OpenDNSSEC and the tools in the BIND distribution can help.

On-the-Fly DNSSEC Signing with the dnssec Plug-in

In addition to signing static zone data, CoreDNS can sign zone data "on the fly." For example, resource records in responses synthesized by the kubernetes plug-in can be signed using DNSSEC. Configuring on-the-fly DNSSEC signing in CoreDNS is done using the dnssec plug-in. Example 7-25 displays its syntax.

Example 7-25. Syntax of dnssec plug-in

```
dnssec [ZONES...] {
    key file KEY...
    cache_capacity CAPACITY
}
```

ZONES lists the zones that will be signed on the fly. Per usual, if not specified, all of the zones in the server block are signed. key file specifies the name of the key file from which to read the cryptographic keys; CoreDNS expects the keys to have been generated using dnssec-keygen (which is why we showed it to you earlier!). You can use the basename or either filename (*basename.key* or *basename.private*) to specify the key file.

CoreDNS will sign generated resource records on the fly with the configured keys. If you configure both a KSK and a ZSK pair, as we generated earlier, CoreDNS will sign DNSKEY records with the KSK private key and all other records using the ZSK private key. If you configure only a single key, without the KSK flag set, CoreDNS will treat it as a Common Signing Key (CSK) and will sign all records with it.

The CoreDNS developers recommend using the ECDSA algorithm with on-the-fly because it generates smaller signatures than other options.

Finally, cache_capacity specifies the size of the cache that the dnssec plug-in uses to store generated signatures. After the dnssec plug-in generates a signature for a particular synthesized resource record, it stores that signature so that it won't need to recalculate the same signature later. The default is 10,000 signatures.

Example 7-26 demonstrates using the dnssec plug-in with the kubernetes plug-in to sign records synthesized from a Kubernetes cluster.

Example 7-26. Example dnssec plug-in

```
cluster.local {
    kubernetes
    dnssec {
      key file Kcluster.local+013+47746
    }
}
```

The `dnssec` plug-in and the previous plug-ins that we've covered implement advanced DNS functionality. Let's take a look at how one company put some of those plug-ins together as a cloud-based DNS service.

Case Study: Infoblox's BloxOne Threat Defense

For a real-world case study of how you can use CoreDNS to interpret requests and manipulate responses, we can look at Infoblox's *BloxOne Threat Defense*.

Infoblox's heritage is in appliances that serve DNS and DHCP on customers' networks. In fact, Infoblox has grown to become the dominant vendor of "DDI" products: DNS, DHCP, and IP Address Management. But DDI products have evolved over the past several years.

With the advent of Response Policy Zones (RPZs), developed by Paul Vixie and Vernon Schryver while they were at the Internet Systems Consortium, customers gained the ability to configure resolution policy on their DNS servers, including Infoblox appliances. They could create rules that would prevent known malicious domain names from being resolved, and prevent any domain name from resolving to IP addresses believed to be malicious. They could subscribe to RPZ "feeds" containing lists of domain names actively being used on the internet for malign purposes, curated by respected internet security organizations such as Spamhaus and SURBL.

However, after their employees began using DNS infrastructure provided by someone other than their employer, all of this protection was lost. Employees working from home or traveling would generally use whichever DNS servers were assigned by DHCP, which lacked the RPZ configuration the their employer had painstakingly set up.

To address this shortcoming, Infoblox developed BloxOne Threat Defense. BloxOne Threat Defense (man, isn't there something we can call that for short?) is a cloud-based recursive DNS service that allows customers to apply a configurable resolution policy to their employees' devices and maintain visibility of their employees' DNS activity while those employees are outside the corporate network.

To do this, BloxOne Threat Defense (how about, "B1TD"?) uses CoreDNS in a couple of different roles: CoreDNS is the heart of the software that sends employees' queries to the B1TD cloud, and CoreDNS also receives those employees' queries in the cloud, checks for applicable policies, and applies them. CoreDNS's plug-ins and plug-in-based architecture make it well suited to both of these very different applications.

Let's begin by examining how CoreDNS is used to determine which user sent a query.

Identifying Users

The first challenge in designing B1TD was determining how to identify individual users. This is necessary to determine which resolution policies to apply to a query and to associate queries and responses with the user who generated them for logging purposes.

By default, DNS messages don't contain any information that can identify an individual user. Sometimes, the IP address from which a query is received can identify the user who sent it, but more often the IP address is dynamic, assigned using DHCP, or a single IP address shared by a set of users behind a device that performs Network Address Translation (NAT). In those cases, the IP address doesn't easily map to a user's identity.

To address this, Infoblox configures the stub resolver on B1TD clients to query a local instance of CoreDNS running on the loopback address. This instance of CoreDNS adds an EDNS0 option to the query it receives using the `rewrite` plug-in. The option contains identifying information about the client (e.g., its MAC address, IP address, and the organization it belongs to) and the user's login name. CoreDNS then forwards this query to the B1TD cloud's anycast address. Because the information added is sensitive, personal data, CoreDNS uses the `forward` plug-in's support for DNS over TLS (DoT) to encrypt communication with the forwarder, as depicted in Figure 7-1.

For cases in which several B1TD clients access the B1TD cloud from a single network or site, Infoblox supplies a *DNS Forwarding Proxy*. The DNS Forwarding Proxy is a virtual machine (VM)-based or container-based instance of CoreDNS that performs the same function as the client-based version, but it can receive queries from a number of clients.

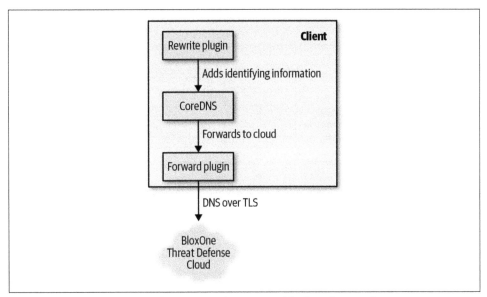

Figure 7-1. CoreDNS using the rewrite plug-in to add identifying information

Now that queries are tagged with identity information, we can apply the correct policy.

Applying Policy

In the cloud, CoreDNS receives a query from either the client-based CoreDNS or the DNS Forwarding Proxy. CoreDNS's small resource footprint enables Infoblox to run many instances behind a load balancer (run as containers, managed by Kubernetes, natch...), and to start and stop instances quickly to accommodate varying load. CoreDNS calls the `policy` plug-in[5] with attributes of the query, including the client's identity and, if provided, the user's identity as well as the domain name being looked up and type requested. The `policy` plug-in identifies the set of policies that apply to the user and returns with information on whether any of those policies applied to the combination of client, user, domain name, and type. If not, CoreDNS forwards the query to an instance of Unbound, a fast DNS server that supports full recursion, and awaits a response. If there is an applicable policy, CoreDNS applies it, generally responding with an error or a redirection to the domain name or IP address of a web-based landing page. Figure 7-2 presents this process.

---

5 The `policy` plug-in was written by Infoblox but hasn't yet made it into CoreDNS. It is open source, however, and is freely downloadable from GitHub (*https://oreil.ly/IDwmZ*).

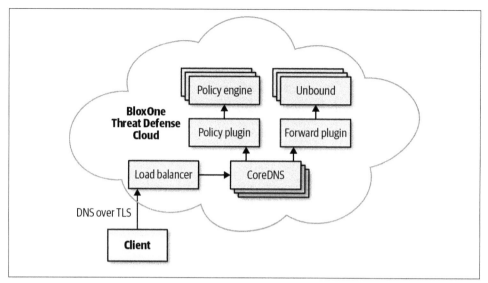

Figure 7-2. CoreDNS in the BloxOne Threat Defense cloud

CoreDNS's versatility allows Infoblox to use it both as the main component of the client and an integral part of the cloud solution. On the client, it requires very few resources and supports rewriting queries (to add identifying information) and forwarding over TLS (to preserve the security of that information). In the cloud, it supports horizontal scaling using Kubernetes and easy extension to functionality using a custom plug-in (`policy`, in this case).

In BloxOne Threat Defense, CoreDNS and its plug-ins are combined to provide a useful service. In Chapter 8, we look at plug-ins that would help us monitor the CoreDNS instances that support that service.

Monitoring and Troubleshooting

Given how critical a service DNS is, it's important to have the ability to monitor its availability and performance and to troubleshoot problems it might be experiencing. In this chapter, we cover plug-ins that will help you monitor CoreDNS, log queries and responses, and diagnose issues.

The prometheus Plug-in

CoreDNS exposes many metrics using the prometheus plug-in. As the name suggests, these are exposed in the format used by the Prometheus monitoring system. The plug-in will open a port for Prometheus or other tools to scrape the metrics periodically.

Example 8-1 presents the complete syntax.

Example 8-1. Syntax of the prometheus plug-in

```
prometheus [ ADDRESS ]
```

ADDRESS is the IP and port to listen on; if omitted it defaults to localhost:9153.

The plug-in will start up an HTTP server with a handler for *metrics*—any other path will result in an HTTP 404 Not Found error. CoreDNS will export basic process and Go runtime metrics as well as CoreDNS-specific metrics, as described in Table 8-1.

Table 8-1. Exported metrics

Name	Labels	Description
process_cpu_seconds_total		Total user and system CPU time spent in seconds
process_open_fds		Number of open file descriptors
process_max_fds		Maximum number of open file descriptors
process_virtual_memory_bytes		Virtual memory size in bytes
process_virtual_memory_max_bytes		Maximum amount of virtual memory available in bytes
process_resident_memory_bytes		Resident memory size in bytes
process_start_time_seconds		Start time of the process since Unix epoch in seconds
go_goroutines		Number of goroutines that currently exist
go_threads		Number of operating system threads created
go_gc_duration_seconds		A summary of the garbage collection invocation durations
go_info	version	Information about the Go environment
go_memstats_alloc_bytes		Number of bytes allocated and still in use
go_memstats_alloc_bytes_total		Total number of bytes allocated, even if freed
go_memstats_sys_bytes		Number of bytes obtained from system
go_memstats_lookups_total		Total number of pointer lookups
go_memstats_mallocs_total		Total number of mallocs
go_memstats_frees_total		Total number of frees
go_memstats_heap_alloc_bytes		Number of heap bytes allocated and still in use
go_memstats_heap_sys_bytes		Number of heap bytes obtained from system
go_memstats_heap_idle_bytes		Number of heap bytes waiting to be used
go_memstats_heap_inuse_bytes		Number of heap bytes that are in use
go_memstats_heap_released_bytes		Number of heap bytes released to OS
go_memstats_heap_objects		Number of allocated objects
go_memstats_stack_inuse_bytes		Number of bytes in use by the stack allocator
go_memstats_stack_sys_bytes		Number of bytes obtained from system for stack allocator
go_memstats_mspan_inuse_bytes		Number of bytes in use by mspan structures
go_memstats_mspan_sys_bytes		Number of bytes used for mspan structures obtained from system
go_memstats_mcache_inuse_bytes		Number of bytes in use by mcache structures
go_memstats_mcache_sys_bytes		Number of bytes used for mcache structures obtained from system
go_memstats_buck_hash_sys_bytes		Number of bytes used by the profiling bucket hash table
go_memstats_gc_sys_bytes		Number of bytes used for garbage collection system metadata

Name	Labels	Description
go_memstats_other_sys_bytes		Number of bytes used for other system allocations
go_memstats_next_gc_bytes		Number of heap bytes when next garbage collection will take place
go_memstats_last_gc_time_seconds		Number of seconds since 1970 of last garbage collection
go_memstats_gc_cpu_fraction		The fraction of this program's available CPU time used by the garbage collection since the program started
coredns_build_info	version, revision, goversion	This metric always has the value 1, but has labels with the CoreDNS version, Git revision, and Go version used to build CoreDNS
coredns_dns_request_count_total	server, zone, proto, family	Counter of DNS requests made per zone, protocol and family
coredns_dns_request_duration_seconds	server, zone	Histogram of the time (in seconds) each request took
coredns_dns_request_size_bytes	server, zone, proto	Histogram of the size of the EDNS0 UDP buffer in bytes (64 K for TCP)
coredns_dns_request_do_count_total	server, zone	Counter of DNS requests with DO bit set per zone
coredns_dns_request_type_count_total	server, zone, type	Counter of DNS requests per type, per zone
coredns_dns_response_size_bytes	server, zone, proto	Histogram of the size of the returned response in bytes
coredns_dns_response_rcode_count_total	server, zone, rcode	Counter of response status codes
coredns_panic_count_total		A metrics that counts the number of panics
coredns_plugin_enabled	server, zone, name	A metric that indicates whether a plug-in is enabled on per-server and per-zone basis

Individual plug-ins can also add metrics to the list. Consult the documentation for those plug-ins for the details.

Metrics can be very useful in understanding how many resources (including CPU) CoreDNS is consuming to handle queries. But what if we want to see individual queries? Enter the log plug-in.

The log Plug-in

The log plug-in allows you to log a message for every query CoreDNS receives. That can be helpful if you're trying to debug a problem (e.g., is CoreDNS in fact receiving a query from the user's computer?) or if you'd like to keep a log of all queries processed for security purposes. In its simplest form, the log plug-in looks like Example 8-2.

Example 8-2. Syntax of the log plug-in

```
log
```

Yup, that's it. Example 8-3 shows the `log` plug-in in use.

Example 8-3. The log plug-in in action

```
. {
    forward . 8.8.8.8 8.8.4.4
    cache 3600
    log
}
```

This instructs CoreDNS to log a message in a default log format for each query received by the server block in which the `log` plug-in appears. Here's an example of a log message:

```
2019-04-26T14:03:32.286-07:00 [INFO] 127.0.0.1:54308 - 31656
"A IN www.nxdomain.com. udp 45 false 4096" NXDOMAIN qr,rd,ra 128 0.172121417s
```

The first field, starting with `2019`, is a timestamp in the format specified in RFC 3339, followed by the severity, and then the IP address (`127.0.0.1`) and port (`54308`) from which the query was received. `31656` is the Message ID of the query, and `A IN www.nxdomain.com.` tells us the query type (`A`), query class (`IN`), and query domain name (`www.nxdomain.com`). The query was received over `udp` and was `45` bytes long, and the DNSSEC OK bit was not set (hence, `false`). The maximum buffer size advertised by the querier was `4096` bytes. The remaining fields pertain to our reply: the Response Code was `NXDOMAIN`, indicating that there is no such domain name as `www.nxdomain.com`. The flags in our response were `qr`, which indicates the message was a response; `rd`, which indicates that the query requested recursion; and `ra`, which means that recursion was available. Finally, the response was `128` bytes long and the query processing (the time it took to answer the query) was about 0.172 seconds.

If you'd prefer to log only queries in certain domains, you can use the syntax shown in Example 8-4.

Example 8-4. Specifying domains in the log plug-in

```
log [NAMES...]
```

`NAMES` is a list of domains for which queries are logged; queries for domain names that don't end in one of the listed domains are not logged. For example, the *Corefile* shown in Example 8-5 would log only queries that ended in `foo.example` or `bar.example`.

Example 8-5. Specifying domains in the log plug-in

```
. {
    forward . 8.8.8.8 8.8.4.4
    log foo.example bar.example
}
```

You can even specify that only queries that generated certain "classes" of responses be logged. Here are the classes:

success
: A successful response.

denial
: A response of NXDOMAIN (again, meaning "there's no such domain name") or NODATA (meaning that there's no data of that type for the specified domain name).

error
: A response of SERVFAIL (Served Failed), NOTIMP (Not Implemented), or REFUSED. These are all indications that the DNS server couldn't respond because of an operational error (SERVFAIL), couldn't process the query because it didn't know how (NOTIMP), or wouldn't answer because of policy, such as an access control list.

all
: All responses.

To specify one or more classes, use the syntax in Example 8-6.

Example 8-6. Specifying classes in the log plug-in

```
log [NAMES...] {
    class CLASSES...
}
```

Example 8-7 demonstrates how to log just denial and error responses to queries in foo.example.

Example 8-7. Indicating specific classes in the log plug-in

```
log foo.example {
    class denial error
}
```

The default is to log all classes.

Finally, the `log` plug-in provides a remarkable amount of control over the format of logged messages. The following fields are available:

`{type}`
Query type.

`{name}`
Query domain name.

`{class}`
Query class.

`{proto}`
Protocol (TCP or UDP).

`{remote}`
The client's IP address. IPv6 addresses are enclosed in brackets, like so: `[::1]`.

`{local}`
The server's IP address. IPv6 addresses are enclosed in brackets.

`{size}`
The query's size in bytes.

`{port}`
The client's port.

`{duration}`
The duration of query processing.

`{rcode}`
The response code (RCODE).

`{rsize}`
The raw (uncompressed) response size.

`{>rflags}`
The flags in the response. Each set flag will be displayed; for example, "qr,rd,ra."

`{>bufsize}`
The buffer size advertised in the query.

`{>do}`
Whether the DNSSEC OK bit was set in the query.

`{>id}`
The message ID.

`{>opcode}`
>   The OPCODE in the query.

`{common}`
>   The Common Log Format (the default).

`{combined}`
>   The Common Log Format plus the query opcode.

The Common Log Format is

```
{remote}:{port} - {>id} "{type} {class} {name} {proto} {size} {>do} {>bufsize}"
{rcode} {>rflags} {rsize} {duration}
```

To specify a log format other than the default Common Log Format, use the format shown in Example 8-8 for the log plug-in:

Example 8-8. Syntax for specifying format in the log plug-in

```
log [NAMES...] [FORMAT]
```

If you want to specify format, you must also specify one or more NAMES, as illustrated in Example 8-9.

Example 8-9. Specifying format in the log plug-in

```
log foo.example "Query: {name} {class} {type}"
```

If you want to log queries for all domain names, use "." as NAMES. And, of course, you can combine NAMES, FORMAT, and CLASSES, as demonstrated in Example 8-10.

Example 8-10. Specifying names, classes, and format in a log plug-in

```
log . "Query: {name} {class} {type}" {
    class success
}
```

CoreDNS's log plug-in provides a very flexible mechanism for logging queries. But what if you want to log more than just the query; for example, a response? You can do that by using the dnstap plug-in, which we cover next.

The dnstap Plug-in

Logging a message for each query received imposes some overhead on a DNS server. As the name suggests, query logging also includes mostly information about the query received but not much about the response to that query (though CoreDNS's log plug-in can include information about some aspects of the response). dnstap was developed to address both of these issues, and provides a mechanism for logging complete response data very efficiently, using minimal resources.

As its website (*http://dnstap.info*) says, dnstap is a flexible, structured, binary log format for DNS. It encodes wire-format DNS messages, so you can see all the details of the responses your DNS server receives. You can collect this information from your DNS infrastructure and mine it later for security, research, and operational purposes, or you can send it to one of many passive DNS databases, where they can do the same.

The dnstap plug-in has a very simple syntax, which you can see in Example 8-11.

Example 8-11. Syntax of the dnstap plug-in

```
dnstap SOCKET [full]
```

SOCKET is either a TCP or Unix domain socket to which CoreDNS will write dnstap information. To specify a TCP socket, use the format tcp://<IP address>:<port>, as shown in Example 8-12.

Example 8-12. The dnstap plug-in with a TCP socket

```
dnstap tcp://127.0.0.1/8053
```

To use a Unix domain socket, you can use the format unix:///path or just path, as illustrated in Example 8-13.

Example 8-13. The dnstap plug-in with a Unix domain socket

```
dnstap unix:///tmp/dnstap.sock
```

Example 8-14 shows its equivalent.

Example 8-14. The dnstap plug-in with a Unix domain socket, take two

```
dnstap /tmp/dnstap.sock
```

The socket is not created by CoreDNS; instead, a different program creates it and listens for dnstap-format information written by CoreDNS (and perhaps other DNS servers). You can find a program for listening to dnstap data (itself called dnstap), as part of the Go language library for working with dnstap data, at *https://github.com/dnstap/golang-dnstap*.

The dnstap program can produce output in JSON, YAML, or an abbreviated text format; read from a file, TCP socket, or a Unix domain socket; and write to standard output or a file. Here's an example of running dnstap to read from a Unix domain socket and writing JSON to standard output:

```
dnstap -j -u /tmp/dnstap.sock -w -
```

The corresponding dnstap plug-in might look like Example 8-15.

Example 8-15. Example dnstap plug-in

```
dnstap /tmp/dnstap.sock
```

Sending a query to CoreDNS might result in output that looks like Example 8-16.

Example 8-16. Example dnstap output

```
% ./dnstap -j -u /tmp/dnstap.sock -w -
dnstap: opened input socket /tmp/dnstap.sock
dnstap.FrameStreamSockInput: accepted a socket connection
{"type":"MESSAGE","message":{"type":"FORWARDER_QUERY",
 "query_time":"2019-04-29T21:14:30.755886Z","socket_family":"INET",
 "socket_protocol":"UDP","response_address":"10.0.2.60","response_port":53}}
{"type":"MESSAGE","message":{"type":"FORWARDER_RESPONSE",
 "response_time":"2019-04-29T21:14:30.755886Z","socket_family":"INET",
 "socket_protocol":"UDP","response_address":"10.0.2.60","response_port":53}}
{"type":"MESSAGE","message":{"type":"CLIENT_QUERY",
 "query_time":"2019-04-29T21:14:30.755977Z","socket_family":"INET",
 "socket_protocol":"UDP","query_address":"127.0.0.1","query_port":62615}}
{"type":"MESSAGE","message":{"type":"CLIENT_RESPONSE",
 "response_time":"2019-04-29T21:14:30.755977Z","socket_family":"INET",
 "socket_protocol":"UDP","query_address":"127.0.0.1","query_port":62615}}
```

You can see when the query was received, when a forwarder was queried, when the forwarder responded, and finally when the response was sent to the client.

To actually see the contents of the query, you need to configure the plug-in to include the wire-format DNS message. Example 8-17 presents a dnstap configuration that writes detailed DNS messages to a TCP socket.

Example 8-17. The dnstap plug-in with full DNS message

```
dnstap tcp://127.0.0.1:8053 full
```

Let's have the dnstap program use YAML output this time, and read from the TCP socket:

```
dnstap -y -l 127.0.0.1:8053 -w -
```

Now we get substantially more output, as shown in Example 8-18.

Example 8-18. The full dnstap output

```
dnstap.FrameStreamSockInput: accepted a socket connection
type: MESSAGE
message:
  type: FORWARDER_QUERY
  query_time: !!timestamp 2019-04-29 21:22:43.146032
  socket_family: INET
  socket_protocol: UDP
  response_address: 10.102.3.10
  response_port: 53
  query_message: |
    ;; opcode: QUERY, status: NOERROR, id: 9193
    ;; flags: rd ad; QUERY: 1, ANSWER: 0, AUTHORITY: 0, ADDITIONAL: 1

    ;; QUESTION SECTION:
    ;berkeley.edu.      IN      SOA

    ;; ADDITIONAL SECTION:

    ;; OPT PSEUDOSECTION:
    ; EDNS: version 0; flags: ; udp: 4096
---
```

As you can see, this output also shows the DNS message header and the contents of the sections of the message. If this had been a response rather than a query, it would have shown the resource records in the response, too.

Both the `log` and `dnstap` plug-ins show the results of successful query processing (though sometimes query processing results in a negative answer or a DNS error). What about errors encountered while processing a query, such as networking problems? We cover that in the next section.

The errors Plug-in

The `errors` plug-in instructs CoreDNS to log any errors encountered during query processing. It's used within a server block, and can be used only once, as demonstrated in Example 8-19.

Example 8-19. The errors plug-in

```
. {
    forward . 8.8.8.8 8.8.4.4
    errors
}
```

errors also allows you to consolidate multiple error messages that match the same regular expression. That way, if CoreDNS is experiencing continuous errors when forwarding queries, for example, you won't be inundated with error messages.

To consolidate error messages, use the syntax shown in Example 8-20.

Example 8-20. Syntax of errors plug-in

```
errors {
    consolidate DURATION REGEXP
}
```

DURATION is a time specification (a number followed by a scaling factor, such a "s" for seconds or "m" for minutes). REGEXP is a double-quoted regular expression that should match a type of error message, such as "^failed to .*" or ".* timeout$". It's recommended to use anchors such as ^ and $ in the regular expression (as in the examples) to improve performance.

Example 8-21 consolidates all "network is unreachable" errors every 10 minutes.

Example 8-21. An errors plug-in with consolidation

```
. {
    forward . 8.8.8.8 8.8.4.4
    errors {
        consolidate 10m ".* network is unreachable$"
    }
}
```

You should also take care not to consolidate too much because the consolidated error message looks like the following:

```
5 errors like '^.* network is unreachable$' occurred in last 10m
```

If you were to use just ".* unreachable$" as the regular expression, you might not be able to tell what the original error messages were about from the consolidated message.

Errors can contribute to slow resolution time, but so can the performance of CoreDNS itself. The trace plug-in, covered next, provides a way to trace the execution times of CoreDNS plug-ins.

The trace Plug-in

The trace plug-in allows you to integrate CoreDNS with distributed tracing tools such as Zipkin, DataDog, and Google's Stackdriver Trace. Distributed tracing systems follow a single request as it moves between sections of code, between microservices, or even between applications.

To enable CoreDNS to trace requests, you just need to include the plug-in. By default, it will use Zipkin for tracing and send traces to `localhost:9411`. The *Corefile* in Example 8-22 will enable tracing for every request.

Example 8-22. Corefile with trace enabled

```
.:5300 {
  trace
  log
  errors
  rewrite class CH IN
  forward . /etc/resolv.conf
}
```

With this *Corefile*, traces will appear in Zipkin, as shown in Figure 8-1.

Figure 8-1. A CoreDNS trace in Zipkin

When using the gRPC Remote Procedure Call (gRPC) protocol, tracing can transit servers. That is, the tracing span identifiers will be carried over the gRPC connection, so you can see how the different services interact, and where the most time is spent. The client span will show all of the different services including DNS lookups to CoreDNS.

There are a couple of caveats with tracing. The first is that it has a dramatic impact on performance. Luckily, CoreDNS offers a way to mitigate this: you can enable tracing only one of every *N* requests. Example 8-23 shows how to do this.

Example 8-23. Tracing only some requests

```
trace {
  every 10000
}
```

This setting instructs CoreDNS to trace only one of every 10,000 requests. This will have a minimal impact on performance, but still provide data as to where time is spent with your requests.

The second caveat has to do with time synchronization across hosts. DNS requests are often very short, often far less than one millisecond. If your request spans multiple hosts, even a few nanoseconds of difference in your clocks can lead to some misleading results; for example, spans that start on the server before they leave the client! Tracing can still provide a useful signal, but it is important to be aware of the caveats.

The complete syntax of the trace plug-in is:

Example 8-24. The complete syntax for the trace plug-in

```
trace [TYPE] [ENDPOINT] {
  every AMOUNT
  service NAME
  client_server
}
```

AMOUNT controls how often traces are done. There will be one trace for every AMOUNT request.

NAME defines the service name to use when sending traces. This defaults to coredns, but if you have multiple CoreDNS instances playing different roles (e.g., one CoreDNS forwarding to another), or different deployments of CoreDNS tracing to the same service, you can provide a name to differentiate them.

If `client_server` is specified, the client and server will share the same span.

The `trace` plug-in can help you diagnose performance problems with CoreDNS. If a problem is causing CoreDNS to crash, though, you might need the `debug` plug-in, which we cover next.

The debug Plug-in

Normally, if CoreDNS crashes, it will restart on its own. Sometimes, however, you might want to inhibit this behavior because you're looking to debug the problem that caused the crash. That's where the `debug` plug-in comes in.

`debug` instructs CoreDNS not to recover from a crash so that you can retrieve the stack trace to help troubleshoot the problem. As a side effect, the `debug` plug-in instructs CoreDNS to send *log.Debug* and *log.Debugf* messages to standard output, which can also help diagnose an issue.

`debug`'s syntax couldn't be simpler, as demonstrated in Example 8-25.

Example 8-25. Syntax of the debug plug-in

```
debug
```

Remember to specify the `debug` plug-in in any server blocks in which you want to produce debug output, as shown in Example 8-26.

Example 8-26. The debug plug-in in action

```
foo.example {
    file /db.foo.example
    errors
    debug
}

. {
    forward . 8.8.8.8 8.8.4.4
    errors
    debug
}
```

Don't Use debug in Production!

Because the `debug` plug-in inhibits the automatic restarting of CoreDNS, you should never use it in production.

This chapter covered several plug-ins useful to DNS server administrators, including `log`, `dnstap`, and `errors`, and some that are more useful to developers, such as `trace` and `debug`. (One of them, `prometheus`, is arguably handy for both administrators and developers.) In Chapter 9, we'll cover how enterprising developers can build their own versions of CoreDNS and write their own plug-ins.

Building a Custom Server

One of the best things about CoreDNS is how easy it is to customize and add new plug-ins. Because of this, there are a wide variety of *external* plug-ins available. By "external," we mean not part of the standard CoreDNS build or repository, and often not even part of the CoreDNS GitHub organization. To utilize external plug-ins, you need to rebuild CoreDNS. Plug-ins are not loaded dynamically, but are instead compiled in at build time.

The CoreDNS code is also structured to make it easy to use as a library. This means that you can create your own main routine and treat the entire CoreDNS code as a library. This chapter covers both of these options.

Compiling CoreDNS with an External Plug-in

The simplest way to build a custom CoreDNS with an external plug-in is to modify only the *plugin.cfg* file and rebuild CoreDNS. This uses the standard CoreDNS main routine. Your binary will behave exactly like an ordinary CoreDNS, except it will include the additional plug-in and its directives.

You do not need to be a Go developer to build custom versions of CoreDNS, but you will need a machine that's set up for doing Go builds. If you have Docker up and running, you can get away with just that. Otherwise, you will need Go 1.12 or later, Git, and Make.

First, let's look at building CoreDNS with only Docker. The examples here will use a Linux machine, but you can also build CoreDNS on Windows.

Building Using Docker

When using Docker, you must first download the CoreDNS source code to a directory on your machine. Rather than installing git, we can use the golang:1.12 Docker image, which includes git, to pull down the repository from GitHub, as shown in Example 9-1. It is not important where this directory is located on your workstation.

This command mounts the current working directory (*$PWD*) as */go* in the container and then runs several commands via bash: the git command to clone the CoreDNS repository into */go/coredns*, change the directory to *coredns*, and switch to the v1.5.0 release tag (the latest as of this writing). Notice the -u $(id -u):$(id -g). This is used to set the user and group inside the container to the current user and group outside the container. Without this, all of the files that are created in the container would be owned by root and thus would not be editable by just any user.

Example 9-1. Retrieving the CoreDNS source code

```
$ docker run --rm -u $(id -u):$(id -g) -v $PWD:/go golang:1.12 \
    /bin/bash -c \
    "git clone https://github.com/coredns/coredns.git && \
    cd coredns && \
    git checkout v1.5.0"
Cloning into 'coredns'...
Note: checking out 'v1.5.0'.

You are in 'detached HEAD' state...
...
HEAD is now at e3f9a80b... WIP: travis changes (#2766)
```

The result of this is a *coredns* directory on your workstation, with the v1.5.0 source code ready to build. We use the golang:1.12 image for that, as well, as shown in Example 9-2. This docker command mounts the source directory in the container, switches to that working directory, and builds CoreDNS with make.

Example 9-2. Building with Docker

```
$ cd coredns
$ docker run --rm -v $PWD:/coredns -w /coredns golang:1.12 make
** presubmit/context
** presubmit/filename-hyphen
** presubmit/import-testing
** presubmit/test-lowercase
** presubmit/trailing-whitespace
...
github.com/openzipkin/zipkin-go-opentracing
github.com/DataDog/dd-trace-go/tracer
```

```
gopkg.in/DataDog/dd-trace-go.v0/opentracing
github.com/coredns/coredns/plugin/trace
github.com/coredns/coredns/core/plugin
github.com/coredns/coredns
$ ls -l coredns
-rwxr-xr-x 1 root root 42204416 May  6 01:23 coredns
```

After this completes, you will have a *coredns* Linux[1] binary in the *coredns* directory. Notice this is owned by `root`; this is because we didn't use the `-u` for the build step. That is necessary because the build will create some directories in places that an ordinary user cannot. Having the executable be owned by `root` is not a problem for us.

The binary we build is a standard binary—without any customization. We look at how to customize the binary in "Modifying plugin.cfg" on page 161.

If you do not want to use Docker to build, the next section explains how to build CoreDNS without Docker.

Building on Your Workstation

Building with Docker works, but it has one big drawback: it is really slow when doing iterative development. Because the build is using Docker, it starts with a fresh container every time and needs to download all of the packages again. We can make this much faster by setting up a local Go development environment.[2]

You will need `git` and `make`; your standard package installer that comes with your system should have recent enough versions of these available. For `go`, you will need version 1.12 or later. Your distribution might not have that recent of a version available. To get the latest, see *https://golang.org/dl/*. To install it, download and unpack it into the */usr/local* directory, as shown in Example 9-3. This example also assumes that you have cURL installed and download the file. The example first checks whether you already have `go` and then downloads and installs it (if you don't) and verifies that it is available. Finally, it creates the Go workspace directory in your *home* directory. If you put it somewhere else, you need to set the `GOPATH` environment variable.

Example 9-3. Installing Go

```
$ which go
$ curl -s https://dl.google.com/go/go1.12.4.linux-amd64.tar.gz \
  | sudo tar -C /usr/local -xz
$ which go
```

---

1 It will be a Linux binary, even if you build on some other platform (such as MacOS). This is because the Docker container that does the build is running Linux.

2 Or you can save intermediate Docker images, but that's not really worth the hassle in the long run.

```
/usr/local/go/bin/go
$ go version
go version go1.12.4 linux/amd64
$ mkdir ~/go
```

In earlier versions of Go, it was necessary to put the CoreDNS source directory in the correct spot based on your GOPATH in order to build. Now, CoreDNS uses *go modules* for dependency management, so this is no longer necessary; you can put the *coredns* directory anywhere and still be able to build.

You will need to use Git to clone the CoreDNS repository, as shown in Example 9-4. This example also shows switching to the v1.5.0 branch, and finally building CoreDNS with Make.

Example 9-4. Cloning and building CoreDNS

```
$ git clone https://github.com/coredns/coredns
Cloning into 'coredns'...
remote: Enumerating objects: 5, done.
remote: Counting objects: 100% (5/5), done.
remote: Compressing objects: 100% (5/5), done.
remote: Total 51401 (delta 0), reused 1 (delta 0), pack-reused 51396
Receiving objects: 100% (51401/51401), 88.33 MiB | 890.00 KiB/s, done.
Resolving deltas: 100% (24734/24734), done.
$ cd coredns
$ git checkout v1.5.0
Note: checking out 'v1.5.0'.
...
HEAD is now at e3f9a80b... WIP: travis changes (#2766)
$ make
** presubmit/context
** presubmit/filename-hyphen
** presubmit/import-testing
** presubmit/test-lowercase
** presubmit/trailing-whitespace
...
github.com/coredns/coredns
$ ls -l coredns
-rwxr-xr-x 1 john john 42212608 May  6 01:40 coredns
```

Now that we know how to build a basic CoreDNS binary, in the next section, we show you how to customize it.

Modifying plugin.cfg

The *plugin.cfg* file is a simple configuration file used to control which plug-ins are compiled into CoreDNS during the build. It consists of one plug-in directive and source directory per line, separated by a colon. Example 9-5 shows a snippet of this file. Modifying this file and rebuilding is the quickest and simplest way to build a custom CoreDNS. It lets you remove any unneeded plug-ins, and add any external or custom plug-ins that you want.

Example 9-5. Plug-in configuration file

```
# Directives are registered in the order they should be
# executed.
#
# Ordering is VERY important. Every plugin will
# feel the effects of all other plugin below
# (after) them during a request, but they must not
# care what plugin above them are doing.

# How to rebuild with updated plugin configurations:
# Modify the list below and run `go gen && go build`

# The parser takes the input format of
#       <plugin-name>:<package-name>
# Or
#       <plugin-name>:<fully-qualified-package-name>
#
# External plugin example:
# log:github.com/coredns/coredns/plugin/log
# Local plugin example:
# log:log

metadata:metadata
cancel:cancel
tls:tls
reload:reload
nsid:nsid
root:root
bind:bind
...
on:github.com/mholt/caddy/onevent
```

As stated in the comment, the order in this file is critical. CoreDNS does not support dynamically reordering plug-ins.[3] So, regardless of the order that directives are listed in the *Corefile*, the plug-in chain will be built in the order in *plugin.cfg*. That is, when

---

3 Yet. Maybe this will happen. It would seem useful, but it adds a lot of complexity to debugging your configuration.

a request is processed by CoreDNS, it will be processed by each plug-in in the order they are defined in this file. Any plug-in earlier in the list can choose to handle the request and return or pass it on to the next plug-in to handle. Not surprisingly, this can be confusing for users, so it might need to change at some point.

Let's try adding in a new plug-in that is not part of v1.5.0.[4] We can enable the any plug-in, a small plug-in that is part of the CoreDNS organization, but is not built-in by default in v1.5.0. It implements RFC 8482, which obsoletes ANY queries, returning only a minimal response. This eliminates one attack method that can be used in DNS amplification attacks.

You can find the code for the CoreDNS any plug-in at *https://github.com/coredns/any*, but it is not critical what the code looks like for this exercise. Instead, we just need to modify *plugin.cfg*. Try putting the line any:github.com/coredns/any on line 24, directly after the line with cancel:cancel, and then run make either directly or using Docker, depending on how you built the binary previously. After you do this, run ./coredns -plugins. You will see the any plug-in listed at the top (these are in alphabetical order), as shown in Example 9-6.

Example 9-6. The any plug-in

```
$ ./coredns -plugins
Server types:
  dns

Caddyfile loaders:
  flag
  default

Other plugins:
  dns.any
  dns.auto
  dns.autopath
  dns.bind
  dns.cache
...
  on
```

If you want to try out this new binary, just create a simple *Corefile* like that shown in Example 9-7 and run CoreDNS with that *Corefile*. It enables the any plug-in and forwards all other queries to Google's 8.8.8.8 public DNS server.

---

4 It has been added in v1.5.1, so these steps work specifically with v1.5.0. The same steps would work with other plug-ins in later versions of CoreDNS.

Example 9-7. Corefile for the any plug-in

```
.:5300 {
  any
  log
  forward . 8.8.8.8
}
```

Example 9-8 shows how CoreDNS responds to an ANY query now, returning a single HINFO record pointing to the RFC. Since the any plug-in comes before the forward plug-in in *plugin.cfg*, it takes the query and replies, never passing the request down the chain to the forward plug-in.

Example 9-8. any comes first

```
$ dig -p 5300 -t ANY example.com @localhost

; <<>> DiG 9.10.3-P4-Debian <<>> -p 5300 -t ANY example.com @localhost
;; global options: +cmd
;; Got answer:
;; ->>HEADER<<- opcode: QUERY, status: NOERROR, id: 12466
;; flags: qr rd; QUERY: 1, ANSWER: 1, AUTHORITY: 0, ADDITIONAL: 1
;; WARNING: recursion requested but not available

;; OPT PSEUDOSECTION:
; EDNS: version: 0, flags:; udp: 4096
;; QUESTION SECTION:
;example.com.                   IN      ANY

;; ANSWER SECTION:
example.com.            8482    IN      HINFO   "ANY obsoleted" "See RFC 8482"

;; Query time: 0 msec
;; SERVER: ::1#5300(::1)
;; WHEN: Tue May 07 00:53:06 UTC 2019
;; MSG SIZE  rcvd: 90
```

To see the effect of ordering in *plugin.cfg*, you can try moving the any line to just after forward, which is line 56 in the original file, and rebuilding CoreDNS. After starting up CoreDNS with the new binary, run the query again and you should see a result like that shown in Example 9-9.

Example 9-9. forward comes first

```
$ dig -p 5300 -t ANY example.com @localhost

; <<>> DiG 9.10.3-P4-Debian <<>> -p 5300 -t ANY example.com @localhost
;; global options: +cmd
;; Got answer:
```

```
;; ->>HEADER<<- opcode: QUERY, status: NOERROR, id: 64826
;; flags: qr rd ra ad; QUERY: 1, ANSWER: 18, AUTHORITY: 0, ADDITIONAL: 1

;; OPT PSEUDOSECTION:
; EDNS: version: 0, flags:; udp: 4096
;; QUESTION SECTION:
;example.com.                    IN      ANY

;; ANSWER SECTION:
example.com.            499     IN      SOA     sns.dns.icann.org. noc.dns.icann...
example.com.            18499   IN      RRSIG   A 8 2 86400 ...
example.com.            18499   IN      RRSIG   NS 8 2 86400 ...
...
```

Of course, `any` is essentially useless when built this way because almost all other plug-ins come before it.

Next, let's take a look at a more extensive change than adding an external plug-in: replacing the `main` function of CoreDNS.

Replacing main

If you need a specialized DNS server that minimizes size and functionality, you could build CoreDNS with only the plug-ins you need enabled in *plugin.cfg*. Sometimes there is additional work that needs to be done that is not part of the standard CoreDNS initialization. In that case, just modifying the *plugin.cfg* is not enough. Instead, you need to create your own `main` function, which can take care of whatever initialization or other processing you need.

CoreDNS is used simply as a library in this case, with your program using it to serve up DNS. This means that you can create a separate repository for your program and just import the parts of CoreDNS you need like any other `go` package. Your program can take its own command-line flags, and can be named something other than `coredns`. If you have many changes, this is much more convenient than having to fork the main CoreDNS repository.

The Kubernetes Node-Local DNS Cache is an upcoming Kubernetes feature[5] that puts a small, custom-built DNS server on each node and uses this technique. That DNS server *is* CoreDNS, but running its own `main` routine that starts up Go routines for the special needs of this use case.

In this section, we show a simple example to make the concept clear. If you want a more complex example, you can see the *cmd/node-cache/main.go* file in the Kubernetes DNS (*https://github.com/kubernetes/dns*) repository.

---

5 This went Alpha in 1.13, and Beta in 1.15. GA is to be determined.

For our example, suppose that we want to run a simple caching DNS server that takes minimal memory, and does not require users to understand *Corefile* formats or anything about CoreDNS at all. We can build a new `main` routine that accepts our own flags, generates the *Corefile*, and then starts up CoreDNS with that *Corefile*.

The learning-coredns (*https://github.com/coredns/learning-coredns*) GitHub repository contains such a program in the *dnscached* directory. You can clone that repository to follow along. There are only three source files, *main.go*, *dnscached.go*, and *dnscached_test.go*. We step through the critical parts in Example 9-10, starting with the entire *main.go*, which is only 38 lines of code.

Example 9-10. dnscached's main.go

```go
package main

import (
        "fmt"
        "os"

        "github.com/mholt/caddy"
)

func init() {
        caddy.Quiet = true // don't show init stuff from caddy
        caddy.AppName = "dnscached"
        caddy.AppVersion = "1.0.0"
}

func main() {
        d := parseFlags()

        d.handleVersion()

        input, err := d.corefile()
        if err != nil {
                fmt.Fprintf(os.Stderr, err.Error())
                os.Exit(1)
        }

        d.handleDryRun(input)

        // Start the server
        instance, err := caddy.Start(input)
        if err != nil {
                fmt.Fprintf(os.Stderr, err.Error())
                os.Exit(1)
        }

        // Twiddle your thumbs
```

```
        instance.Wait()
}
```

After the standard system imports, notice that we import `github.com/mholt/caddy`.[6] Recall that CoreDNS uses the Caddy framework to do all of the basic server management: configuration, startup, graceful restart, reload, and shutdown. We will need some functions from this library to set up the configuration and start the server.

The `init` function just configures Caddy to not emit its normal startup and initialization output, and stores the name and version of this application in the Caddy variables for later use. This is a simple best practice when building custom, CoreDNS-based binaries like this.

Here is the basic flow[7] of the `main` function:

1. Parse the flags, creating a `dnscached` struct (defined in *dnscached.go*).
2. Use that struct to generate the *Corefile* in memory.
3. Start up the server with that *Corefile*.
4. Simply wait for the server to exit (which will be never, unless you implement some special signal handling).

The call to `caddy.Start` returns a `caddy.Instance`, which contains all of the state of the running server. This includes lists of callbacks to be executed during different server life cycle events, such as startup, restart, and shutdown. You can register those handlers during parsing of the *Corefile*, which we explore in "Writing a Custom Plugin" on page 170.

The *dnscached.go* file contains the logic used to parse and handle the various flags and to generate the *Corefile* that will be used to start the server. It is about 140 lines of code, so we will just show the most important parts here; you can get the rest from the GitHub repository. Example 9-11 shows the imports for this file.

Example 9-11. Imports for dnscached

```
import (
        "bytes"
        "flag"
        "fmt"
        "os"

        _ "github.com/coredns/coredns/plugin/bind"
        _ "github.com/coredns/coredns/plugin/cache"
```

---

6 Later versions of Caddy are located at *github.com/caddyserver/caddy*.

7 The `handleVersion` and `handleDryRun` just implement some specific command-line flags and will cause the program to exit.

```
 _ "github.com/coredns/coredns/plugin/errors"
 _ "github.com/coredns/coredns/plugin/forward"
 _ "github.com/coredns/coredns/plugin/log"

 "github.com/mholt/caddy"
)
```

The standard library imports are not interesting, but look at the imports from the CoreDNS repository. We have listed each individual plug-in we need here (unnamed imports using _ because we won't call anything on them). Doing this minimizes the plug-ins built in to our binary, and therefore its size on disk and in memory. If we wanted all the default plug-ins as set in the default *plugin.cfg*, we would import github.com/coredns/coredns/core/plugin, instead, which references all of them.

There are a few functions called from main that we examine here. The first is parseFlags, which was used to create the dnscached structure. Example 9-12 shows the definition of that structure and the parseFlags function.

Example 9-12. Defining and creating the dnscached struct

```
type dnscached struct {
        printVersion, dryRun, enableLog bool
        bindIP                          string
        port, ttl, prefetchAmount       uint
        successSize, denialSize         uint
        destinations                    []string
}

func parseFlags() *dnscached {
        d := &dnscached{}
        f := flag.NewFlagSet(os.Args[0], flag.ExitOnError)
        f.StringVar(&caddy.PidFile, "pidfile", "", "File `path` to write pid file")
        f.BoolVar(&d.printVersion, "version", false, "Show version")
        f.BoolVar(&d.dryRun, "dry-run", false,
                "Prints out the internally generated Corefile and exits")
        f.BoolVar(&d.enableLog, "log", false, "Enable query logging")
        f.StringVar(&d.bindIP, "bind", "127.0.0.1 ::1", "`IP(s)` to which to bind")
        f.UintVar(&d.port, "port", 5300, "Local port `number` to use")
        f.UintVar(&d.successSize, "success", 9984,
                "Number of success cache `entries`")
        f.UintVar(&d.denialSize, "denial", 9984, "Number of denial cache `entries`")
        f.UintVar(&d.prefetchAmount, "prefetch",
                10, "Times a query must be made per minute to qualify for prefetch")
        f.UintVar(&d.ttl, "ttl", 60,
                "Maximum `seconds` to cache records, zero disables caching")

        f.Usage = func() {
                fmt.Fprintf(os.Stderr,
                        "USAGE\n-----\n%s [ options ] [ destinations ]\n",
                        os.Args[0])
```

```
                fmt.Fprintf(os.Stderr, "\nOPTIONS\n-------\n")
                flag.PrintDefaults()
                fmt.Fprintf(os.Stderr, "\nDESTINATIONS\n-----------")
                fmt.Fprintf(os.Stderr, `
One or more forwarding destinations. Each can be a file in /etc/resolv.conf
format or a destination IP or IP:PORT, with or without a with or without a
protocol (leading "PROTO://"), with "dns" and "tls" as the supported PROTO
values. If omitted, "dns" is assumed as the protocol. The default destination is
/etc/resolv.conf.
`)
        }

        flag.CommandLine = f
        flag.Parse()
        d.destinations = flag.Args()
        if len(d.destinations) == 0 {
                d.destinations = []string{"/etc/resolv.conf"}
        }

        return d
}
```

This example demonstrates two things. First, the best practice to use a structure to capture all of your flag values, rather than global variables. This makes building tests that utilize those flags much easier. See *dnscached_test.go* in the same directory for an example of how that structure is used for unit testing.[8]

The second thing the example demonstrates is how to use customized flags in a program that is importing CoreDNS as a library. The parseFlags function creates a new flag.FlagSet. This allows the dnscached program to exclude any flags that are defined by imported code, such as the Caddy libraries or the Kubernetes client-go libraries. Without this, the flags of any imports would be intermingled with your custom flags, causing confusion or even crashing the program.

After creating the new flag.FlagSet and configuring the flags to set values within the dnscached structure, the example also sets the Usage function of the FlagSet so that users get a useful message. This is particularly important if the command takes positional arguments and not just flags, as dnscached does for the forwarding destinations. Finally, in order to create the dnscached structure, the global flag.Command Line is set to the new FlagSet and the flags are parsed with flag.Parse. When the parseFlags function returns, the dnscached structure is completely ready for use.

---

8 It would be even better to split the actual parsing out, so that command-line strings could be used in another set of tests to generate the dnscached structure. That, as they say, is left as an exercise for the reader.

The main function also calls `handleVersion` and `handleDryRun`, but those are straightforward, so we don't cover them here. The last function is `corefile`, which has a `dnscached` pointer as its receiver. This function interprets the options on the `dnscached` structure and creates a *Corefile* in memory to configure the server's behavior. Example 9-13 presents an abridged version of the function.

Example 9-13. The corefile method

```
func (d *dnscached) corefile() (caddy.Input, error) {
        var b bytes.Buffer
        _, err := b.WriteString(fmt.Sprintf(".:%d {\n errors\n bind %s\n",
                d.port, d.bindIP))
        if err != nil {
                return nil, err
        }

// ...many conditional statements building the Corefile string...

        _, err = b.WriteString("\n}\n")
        if err != nil {
                return nil, err
        }

        return caddy.CaddyfileInput{
                Contents:       b.Bytes(),
                Filepath:       "<flags>",
                ServerTypeName: "dns",
        }, nil
}
```

This function creates a buffer and then simply writes out a *Corefile* to that buffer. It also formats the *Corefile* for readability, so that it can be output by the `-dry-run` option. Although it is technically possible to construct a server directly in code, it is not easy and would repeat a lot of Caddy code. Feeding a string version of a *Corefile* to Caddy when we call `caddy.Start` in the `main` function is much simpler. This `corefile` function creates and returns a `caddy.CaddyfileInput`, which is the argument needed by `caddy.Start`.

The last few lines of the `corefile` method shows how the `caddy.CaddyfileInput` structure is created, which requires three fields. The `Contents` is set to the bytes of the *Corefile*, and the `Filepath` to the fixed string `"<flags>"`. The `Filepath` field is used only for debugging—it is for human consumption and so its value just needs to be suggestive of the source of the `Contents`. The `ServerTypeName`, however, is used by Caddy and must be set to `"dns"` in order for the CoreDNS server to be properly created.

The dnscached directory does not contain a Makefile. Instead, it can be built with go build. Example 9-14 shows building and running dnscached with the default settings. Be sure you cd in to the *dnscached* directory that you cloned, before running the example.

Example 9-14. Building and running dnscached

```
$ go build
$ ./dnscached -dry-run
.:5300 {
 errors
 bind 127.0.0.1 ::1
 cache 60 {
  success 9984
  denial 9984
  prefetch 10
 }
 forward . /etc/resolv.conf
}
$ ./dnscached
.:5300 on 127.0.0.1
.:5300 on ::1
```

Now that you understand the basics of adding external plug-ins and of creating your own, specialized version of CoreDNS, let's take a look at how to build a brand new plug-in.

Writing a Custom Plug-in

Changing the plug-ins or adding your own main routine handles some use cases, but it does not let you manipulate DNS requests and responses. To do that, you need to write your own plug-in.

Plug-ins can be roughly categorized into *backends*, *mutators*, and *configurators*. Backends provide data from an original source, such as a file, external database, or other API, or make it up completely. The file plug-in and kubernetes plug-in are clear examples of this. Mutators modify the inbound request, the outbound response, or both. The rewrite plug-in is clearly a mutator; caching plug-ins can also be considered mutators because they retrieve data from other downstream plug-ins. Configurators simply modify the internal behavior of CoreDNS; bind and log plug-ins, for example. This is just a rough model—a plug-in can do any and all of these things. As a best practice, though, a plug-in should follow the Unix philosophy of doing one thing and doing it well. That makes it as reusable as possible.

Writing a CoreDNS plug-in is pretty simple. You need to implement only four functions: init, setup, Name, and ServeDNS. If you are writing a configurator plug-in, your ServeDNS can be just a single line.

The init function does what it says: it performs one-time initialization of the plug-in. This is a standard Go package initialization function, not a specific Caddy or Core-DNS function. For plug-ins, this typically just means calling Caddy functions to register the plug-in's configuration directive, and associate it with the setup function. This instructs Caddy to call the setup function with all *Corefile* contents related to this directive.

The setup function is used to parse the plug-in configuration from the *Corefile*. It will be called exactly once for each server block in which it appears. Each server block in the *Corefile* is represented in this code with a Config object.[9] The setup function will add a Handler to the Config object for the server block, at least for backend and mutator plug-ins. This adds the plug-in into the "plug-in chain"—the sequence of plug-ins through which requests pass, configured for that server block.[10]

Some plug-ins can appear more than once in the *Corefile*, or even in the same server block. When called, the setup function will be passed to all of the data associated with each of its directives in the block, but only in that block. The other blocks are handled with separate calls to setup. The caddy.Controller provides methods to parse these directives in the order they appear in the block. This is explained in more detail during the discussion of our example plug-in in "There Can Be Only One" on page 173.

The setup function is also the place where connections to remote servers or other one-time instantiations can be done, typically by creating callbacks using the caddy.Controller life cycle hooks. Because the setup method is called during parsing of the *Corefile*, and can be called repeatedly, using the life cycle hooks provides the most control over managing any ancillary resources. Table 9-1 describes each of the available hooks.

---

9 If a server block applies to multiple zones (e.g., foo.com bar.com { ...server block...}), internally each of these is treated as separate server blocks, and so the setup will be called in the same way it would be if there were multiple server blocks, one for each zone.

10 Friendly reminder: this is a fixed, compile-time ordering based on *plugin.cfg*.

Table 9-1. Caddy instance life cycle hooks

Controller function	Registers a callback that will be called...
OnFirstStartup	Just before starting the server, but only once at the beginning of the process startup. That is, it is called only for the first Instance created, not for subsequent Instances created during restarts.
OnStartup	Just before starting the server, during both initial startup and restarts.
OnRestart	Just before starting the server, only on restarts.
OnRestartFailed	If a server restart fails.
OnShutdown	Just before stopping the server during restarts and termination of the process.
OnFinalShutdown	Just before stopping the server during termination of the process.

When opening connections to servers, or opening local ports, care must be taken to properly handle restart events in particular. When CoreDNS receives a SIGUSR1 or a SIGHUP, it reloads the *Corefile*, which causes a graceful restart of the server. Internally, a new caddy.Instance is created with the new *Corefile*, and the file descriptors of the listening sockets are handed over to it. In this case, your plug-in OnShutdown, OnStartup, and OnRestart hooks will be called; if the restart subsequently fails, the OnRestartFailed hooks will be called. These are all called before OnShutdown—so there are in fact two caddy.Instances running during this time. Be sure to properly hand off any open ports, rather than attempting to open them anew, which will fail.

The Name and ServeDNS functions implement the Handler interface, which is what the interface used to manage and pass requests through to your plug-in. Name is as simple as it comes, just returning a string with the name of the plug-in, but ServeDNS is the heart of any backend or mutator plug-in, performing the actual query and response manipulation.

ServeDNS accepts a DNS request and a reference to the response socket. It can write a response to that socket, or it can pass the request to the next plug-in. For backend plug-ins, this is straightforward—it creates the records requested based on the query, and writes the response back to the passed-in ResponseWriter object.

For mutator plug-ins, often you need to manipulate response provided by a plug-in later in the chain. For this, the ServeDNS method will sometimes use the "nonwriter" ResponseWriter (github.com/coredns/plugin/pkg/nonwriter) in order to capture a downstream plug-in's response and manipulate it. In the next section, we build a plug-in to demonstrate this.

ServeDNS returns two values: an int and an error. The error is a standard Go error; in case of an error, it should be returned with information to help the user and for logging by the errors plug-in. The int can take on values of a dns.ResponseCode. In particular, this is used to indicate to the server and to earlier plug-ins whether a response has been written to the client socket. If plugin.ClientWrite returns true for the value, a response has not been written so the server or plug-in should write it out.

The `plugin.ClientWrite` will return true for all RCODES, *except*:

- `dns.RcodeServerFailure`
- `dns.RcodeRefused`
- `dns.RcodeFormatError`
- `dns.RcodeNotImplemented`

There Can Be Only One

For an example, we will build a mutator plug-in that takes a response with multiple resource records and trims it down to be a response that has exactly one record of each type. If the plug-in chain returns a response with five A records, the final response that goes to the client will contain only a single A record.

Example 9-15 presents the syntax for this `onlyone` plug-in.

Example 9-15. Syntax of the onlyone plug-in

```
onlyone [ZONES...] {
    types TYPES
}
```

The `types` subdirective defines the types that should be trimmed and can be omitted; it will default to A and AAAA. If `ZONES` is omitted, it will apply to the zones defined for the server block.

Because this will be an external plug-in, start by creating an empty repository and directory, *only-one*, in your GitHub account, and copying files from *https://github.com/coredns/learning-coredns/plugins/only-one*. Alternatively, you can fork *https://github.com/coredns/learning-coredns* repository on GitHub, and work on your fork. Either way, let's look at the files needed in the *only-one* directory:

- *README.md* provides the documentation for the plug-in. It should follow some specific conventions that will make it easy for CoreDNS users to understand how your plug-in works. It is also necessary in order to appear on the External Plug-ins page of *coredns.io*, or to eventually become an in-tree plug-in.
- *setup.go* contains the `init` and `setup` functions, and any helper functions they need.
- *onlyone.go* contains the definition of the `onlyone` struct, the `Name` function, and the `ServeDNS` function and its helpers.
- *setup_test.go* and *onlyone_test.go* contain the unit tests for this code.

First, we will look at the init function, which is shown in Example 9-16.

Example 9-16. init function

```go
func init() {
        caddy.RegisterPlugin("onlyone", caddy.Plugin{
                ServerType: "dns",
                Action:     setup,
        })
}
```

As mentioned, this simply calls Caddy and registers the onlyone directive to instanti-ate a DNS plug-in (ServerType: "dns") and call the setup function, as shown in Example 9-17.

Example 9-17. setup function

```go
func setup(c *caddy.Controller) error {
        t, err := parse(c)
        if err != nil {
                return plugin.Error("onlyone", err)
        }

        dnsserver.GetConfig(c).AddPlugin(func(next plugin.Handler) plugin.Handler {
                t.Next = next
                return t
        })

        return nil
}
```

The **setup** function is also very straightforward. When called during *Corefile* parsing, it is passed a pointer to a caddy.Controller, which can be used to parse the plug-in's configuration from the *Corefile*. It passes the caddy.Controller to the parse func-tion, which is shown in Example 9-18. The parse function returns an onlyone struct, defined in *onlyone.go*, which contains the configuration of this instance of our plug-in. That struct is also a receiver for the Name and ServeDNS functions, meaning that it implements the plugin.Handler interface.

The parse function handles the syntax shown in Example 9-15. It does this by looping through the directives (the c.Next loop), getting the zones for the directive, and then looping through any defined subdirectives in the c.NextBlock loop.

Example 9-18. parse function

```go
func parse(c *caddy.Controller) (*onlyone, error) {
        o := &onlyone{types: typeMap{dns.TypeA: true, dns.TypeAAAA: true},
                pick: rand.Intn}

        found := false
        for c.Next() {
                // onlyone should just be in the server block once
                if found {
                        return nil, plugin.ErrOnce
                }
                found = true

                // parse the zone list, normalizing each to a FQDN, and
                // using the zones from the server block if none are given.
                args := c.RemainingArgs()
                if len(args) == 0 {
                        o.zones = make([]string, len(c.ServerBlockKeys))
                        copy(o.zones, c.ServerBlockKeys)
                }
                for _, str := range args {
                        o.zones = append(o.zones, plugin.Host(str).Normalize())
                }

                for c.NextBlock() {
                        switch c.Val() {
                        case "types":
                                args := c.RemainingArgs()
                                if len(args) == 0 {
                                        return nil, errors.New(
                                                "at least one type must be listed")
                                }
                                o.types = make(typeMap, len(args))
                                for _, a := range args {
                                        t, ok := dns.StringToType[strings.ToUpper(a)]
                                        if !ok {
                                                return nil,
                                                        fmt.Errorf("invalid type %q",
                                                                a)
                                        }
                                        o.types[t] = true
                                }
                        default:
                                return nil, fmt.Errorf("invalid option %q", c.Val())
                        }
                }
        }
        return o, nil
}
```

There is one tricky bit about the parse function: the c.Next function can return true, in which case it will iterate through the loop again. In fact, if the onlyone directive appears multiple times in the server block, c.Next will return true until all of those have been consumed.

In other words, the outer loop with c.Next will loop through all appearances of onlyone, in the order in which they appear in the server block (remember, setup is called another time if onlyone appears in a different server block). The inner loop on c.NextBlock is entered only if the onlyone is followed by a block definition enclosed in curly braces. In that case, it will loop through each line until it reaches the closing brace, as long as you call c.RemainingArgs to consume the tokens on the rest of the line.[11] Because using the onlyone plug-in more than once in the same server block doesn't make any sense, we check for this using the found variable, and if we find it, we return the standard plugin.ErrOnce error.

After the plug-in data is parsed and we have created an onlyone struct and Handler, the setup function adds it to the list of plug-ins for this server block using GetConfig(c).AddPlugin. Notice that what that function actually receives is a another function, which is used to set the next plug-in in the chain. That is because all of this setup is done during parsing the *Corefile*. The actual plug-in chain is not instantiated until the internal dns.Server is created. This means that if your plug-in needs to know about the existence of other plug-ins in the chain (e.g., metadata, met rics, and ready all need this), they must use the OnStartup hook, or they might miss some that come after them in the *plugin.cfg*.

The plug-in object is now created and registered in the plug-in change. Finally, we will look at the ServeDNS function shown in Example 9-19 to see how it works to manipulate the response.

Example 9-19. The ServeDNS function

```
func (o *onlyone) ServeDNS(ctx context.Context, w dns.ResponseWriter,
        r *dns.Msg) (int, error) {
    // The request struct is a convenience struct.
    state := request.Request{W: w, Req: r}

    // If the zone does not match one of ours, just pass it on.
    if plugin.Zones(o.zones).Matches(state.Name()) == "" {
            return plugin.NextOrFailure(o.Name(), o.Next, ctx, w, r)
    }
```

---

11 The learning-coredns repository contains the plug-in setupcheck to demonstrate this, if you would like to play with it to help your understanding.

```
        // The zone matches ours, so use a nonwriter to capture the response.
        nw := nonwriter.New(w)

        // Call the next plugin in the chain.
        rcode, err := plugin.NextOrFailure(o.Name(), o.Next, ctx, nw, r)
        if err != nil {
                // Simply return if there was an error.
                return rcode, err
        }

        // Now we know that a successful response was received from a plugin
        // that appears later in the chain. Next is to examine that response
        // and trim out extra records, then write it to the client.
        w.WriteMsg(o.trimRecords(nw.Msg))
        return rcode, err
}
```

First, the ServeDNS method creates a request.Request object called state. This is a struct that has a number of convenience methods, and is often useful to create in your ServeDNS method; using state as the name makes it consistent with all of the in-tree plug-ins.

We need to check that the question in the query contains a name that falls within the zones that the plug-in is configured to act upon. The plugin.Zones([]string) function returns an object with a Matches function made just for this purpose. This Matches function will return true if the passed in state.Name() falls within one of the configured zones. If it does not, we just call and return the response from the next plug-in in the chain, using plugin.NextOrFailure.

For queries that match, the ServeDNS function continues by creating the special ResponseWriter with nonwriter.New, and then passes that onto the next plug-in's ServeDNS function. After that plug-in call returns, if there is no error, the response will be stored in the Msg field of the nonwriter we passed in. This is the original response—we next call the trimRecords function to strip out the extra records according to our plug-in's logic.[12] The result of that function is simply written back to the client by calling WriteMsg on the original ResponseWriter that was passed into our ServeDNS.

To try out this plug-in, you need to modify the *plugin.cfg* for CoreDNS, as described in "Modifying plugin.cfg" on page 161. One catch though: during build, go will pull down the plug-in module code from GitHub. To avoid this and instead use the code from your workstation, you need to add a replace directive to your *go.mod* for CoreDNS. This directive will tell go to use a local package directory instead of pulling

---

12 The trimRecords function does not contain CoreDNS-specific code and so is not detailed here, but it is in the *onlyone.go* file in GitHub.

from GitHub. For example, if your plug-in is stored in */home/learning-coredns/ plugins/onlyone*, the `replace` directive to use is `replace github.com/coredns/ learning-coredns/plugins/onlyone => /home/learning-coredns/plugins/ onlyone`. This will allow you to play with the code and rebuild with your modifications.

We now have a functioning plug-in—hooray! The next section discusses how to make that plug-in a supportable and fully functional member of the "plug-in family."

Integrating with Metrics, Trace, and Metadata

To support running your plug-in in production, it is important to provide visibility into its usage and health. Integrating with the *metrics* (`prometheus`) plug-in allows you to export plug-in-specific internal metrics, and integration with the *trace* plug-in allows you to send timing and other data to a distributed tracing service. The `metadata` plug-in allows you to selectively expose data for logging, tracing, or policy use.

To integrate with metrics, use standard Prometheus client libraries. As part of your `OnStartup` calls, you must register your metrics with the Prometheus libraries. A good example of how to do this is with the `template` plug-in, and Example 9-20 shows a snippet from that plug-in's *metrics.go* file that defines a metric.

Example 9-20. Defining a metric for Prometheus

```
templateMatchesCount = prometheus.NewCounterVec(prometheus.CounterOpts{
        Namespace: plugin.Namespace,
        Subsystem: "template",
        Name:      "matches_total",
        Help:      "Counter of template regex matches.",
}, []string{"server", "zone", "class", "type"})
```

Plug-ins should use `plugin.Namespace` for the `Namespace`, and the plug-in name for the `Subsystem`. The `Name` here can be freely chosen, but it should conform to the conventions laid out by the Prometheus project (*https://oreil.ly/JdBK0*). The highlights of this are as follows:

- Must measure the same thing across all values of the labels.
- Must use the same units in all cases.
- Should end in a suffix with the unit name, in plural.
- Should use the base units, which are seconds for time, bytes for memory, and total for accumulating counts. Other values can be found on the Prometheus site.

The Help should be short and descriptive so users know what the metric means. Finally, the list of strings following this are the labels. Typically this includes the server, the zone, and any other plug-in-specific values that you want to include. Be careful, though, because it can greatly increase the amount of data stored if you use too many labels or label values that have too high a cardinality. This can increase the cost of storing and processing the metrics or even overwhelm your metrics system.

This `templateMatchesCount` package variable is then registered with Prometheus (along with some others) through an `OnStartup` hook, as shown in Example 9-21.

Example 9-21. Registering a metric with Prometheus

```
c.OnStartup(func() error {
        metrics.MustRegister(c, templateMatchesCount,
                templateFailureCount, templateRRFailureCount)
        return nil
})
```

Normally this `OnStartup` call will be made from your `setup` function. The metrics package here refers to `github.com/coredns/coredns/plugin/metrics`, which must be imported for this to work.

In contrast, integrating with the `trace` plug-in is quite simple, at least for most plug-ins. In fact, most plug-ins need to do exactly nothing. The `plugin.NextOrFailure` function that most plug-ins use to call the next plug-in takes care of basic integration. This function will create a new `Span` for each plug-in. If you want to add your own `Spans` for your code, see the code for the `forward` plug-in, which does this to track the duration of the connect routines.

Integrating with `metadata` allows your plug-in to present additional values that can be used in the `log`, `firewall`, and other plug-ins. Usage of metadata within `trace`, for example, is under development. This is a relatively new feature whose usefulness will grow as it is adopted by other plug-ins.

To make your plug-in's metadata available, you need to implement the `metadata.Provider` interface. This consists of a single function, `Metadata`, that accepts the same parameters as `ServeDNS` and returns a `context.Context`. When metadata processing is enabled, a call will be made near the start of the plug-in chain execution (by the `metadata` plug-in, in fact) to the `Metadata` method of every plug-in in the chain. This allows each plug-in to add data to the `Context`, before it is passed on to `ServeDNS`.

Given that the `Metadata` function is called on every plug-in for every request matching the `metadata` plug-in's zones, it must be fast. Processing should be minimized. To help this, actual values of the metadata are not stored in the `Context`. Instead, a function that can be used to retrieve the value is stored. If that particular metadata is never used by a consumer (such as `log`), its value function will never be called.

Example 9-22 shows an example of a simple (useless) `Metadata` function that adds a single metadata value to the `Context`.

Example 9-22. A simple Metadata function

```
func (p *myplugin) Metadata(ctx context.Context,
        state request.Request) context.Context {
    metadata.SetValueFunc(ctx, "myplugin/foo", func() string {
        return state.Name()
    })
    return ctx
}
```

This is useless because the query name is already available to any consumer, but it does demonstrate the basic process. This would enable the `log` plug-in to use this value via a log template like `{/myplugin/foo}`, as shown in Example 9-23.

Example 9-23. log plug-in with metadata

```
log foo.example "Query: {name} {class} {type} {/myplugin/foo}"
```

With these last changes integrating metrics, tracing, and metadata with your plug-in, it will now function just as well as any built-in plug-in.

In this chapter, you learned how to customize CoreDNS to serve your own specialized needs. Those customizations can be simply rebuilding while including external plug-ins, building your own specialized DNS server, or adding new backend or mutator plug-ins to upstream CoreDNS. This ability to customize is one of the most powerful features of CoreDNS, and you are now equipped to take advantage of it.

This book has covered a great deal of DNS and CoreDNS material, starting with a refresher on DNS, and going into the basic use and configuration of CoreDNS. You have learned how to use CoreDNS in traditional environments for standard DNS, and for service discovery in virtualized and containerized environments. We hope that the in-depth analysis of the Kubernetes integration will help you support and operate the DNS in your clusters with the best performance and availability. Finally, you learned how to use the advanced features of CoreDNS to manipulate DNS requests and responses, and even how to build your own custom CoreDNS features.

We hope that this knowledge helps you in your daily work. As an open source project, contributions to CoreDNS are always welcome and appreciated. You are invited to join us and the other authors of CoreDNS on GitHub, and we look forward to your participation in making CoreDNS an even better DNS server.

Index

hypervisors, 2

I

ignore empty_service option, 118
imperative APIs, 78
import directive
    importing files into Corefile, 35
    inserting reusable snippet into another part
        of Corefile, 35
IN (internet) class, resource records, 9
in-addr.arpa domain, 23
incremental zone transfers (IXFRs), 41
Infoblox's BloxOne Threat Defense, case study,
    137-140
    applying policy, 139
    identifying users, 138
infoblox/dnstools container image, 83
init function, 171
inline host table entries, 61
intent-based APIs, 78
    (see also declarative APIs)
IP, 3
    cluster IP services in Kubernetes, 80
IP addresses, 3
    A records for IPv4 addresses, 17
    AAAA records for IPv6 addresses, 18
    mapping back to domain name, 23
    user identification and, 138
ip6.arpa domain, 23
iptables, 81

J

JSON
    output of dnstap program, 149
    SkyDNS messages, 70

K

k8s_external plug-in, 117
key rollovers, 132
Key-Signing Key (KSK) pair, generating, 132
key–value stores, 69
    (see also etcd)
kube-dns service, 100
kube-proxy, 81
kubectl client program, 78
kubelet, 79
Kubernetes, 1, 75, 77-119
    autoscaling for CoreDNS deployed in, 105

basic concepts, 77-79
cluster DNS Deployment resources, 98-105
    defining Deployment resource, 101-105
    role-based access control, 98-100
    service, kube-dns, 100
CoreDNS default configuration, 93-96
CoreDNS integration with, 91-93, 109
    (see also kubernetes plug-in)
    better configuration, 106-109
    CoreDNS extensons, 111-118
criticality of CoreDNS to, 4
DNS specification, 82-91
exposing services external to the cluster, 116
integration of CoreDNS with, reasons for,
    77
networking services, 79-82
    Cluster IP, 80
    headless services, 81
Node-Local DNS Cache, 164
stub domains and federations, 96-97
kubernetes plug-in
    complete configuration sytnax, 109
    configuration, 109-111
    how it works, 91
    modifying available records, 117
    support for wildcard queries, 112
    zone transfers, enabling in transfer to
        option, 115

L

labels in Corefile entries, 33
labels option, 118
lifecycle hooks, 171
Linux
    downloading and installing CoreDNS, 31
    iptables utility, 81
liveness probe, CoreDNS container in Kuber-
    netes, 105
load balancing
    in Kubernetes, client-side, 81, 83
    networking service in Kubernetes, 79
loadbalance plug-in, 96
local EDNS0 type, 127
log plug-in, 47, 51, 143-147
    defining reusable snippet for in secondary
        DNS server, 53
    example log message, 144
    fields controlling format of logged messages,
        146

forward, 42-44
independent plug-in chains for zones listed
   at front of server block, 107
root, 39
secondary, 40
writing custom plug-in, 170-180
   integrating with metrics, trace, and
      metadata, 178-180
   onlyone plug-in, 173-178
plugin.cfg file, modifying, 161-164, 177
pods (Kubernetes), 78
   pod options in CoreDNS, 111
   pod template in CoreDNS Deployment
      resource in Kubernetes, 102
   PodSpec, A records and, 85
   resolv.conf file for, 113
   running dnstools pod, 83
   watching pods, autopath plug-in, 109
policy plug-in, 139
policy subdirective (forward plug-in), 43
ports (nondefault), configuring CoreDNS
   server to listen on, 36
prefetching of cached data, 45
primary DNS server, 10
   sample configuration, 52
   setting up for zone or zones, 39
Prometheus
   defining a metric for, 178
   metrics port, 101
   registering metrics with, 179
prometheus plug-in, 95, 141-143
   metrics, 141
   syntax, 141
protocols
   forwarding queries with forwarder plug-in,
     43
   specifying for query processing, 37
PTR (pointer) records, 10, 60
   contents of, 23
   creation of from host table entries, inhibit-
     ing, 61
   queries for, answering with template plug-
     in, 121
   requests for, in kubernetes plug-in, 94

Q

queries and responses, manipulating, 121-140
   case study, Infoblox's BloxOne Threat
     Defense, 137-140

signing responses with DNS Security Extensions, 130-137
using metadata plug-in, 129-130
using rewrite plug-in, 124-129
   for EDNS0 options, 127-128
using template plug-in, 121-123
query processing, 37
quorum, 69

R

RDATA (record-specific data), 10, 17
RDATA format (SOA records), 24
readiness probe, CoreDNS container in Kubernetes, 105
ready plug-in, 105, 107
reconciliation loops (Kubernetes), 78
recursion
   defined, 14
   full, not suppported by CoreDNS, 3
referrals, 13
refresh interval (SOA records), 25
regular expressions
   in errors plug-in, 151
   in rewrite plug-in, 125, 126
   searching for zone data files in auto plug-in,
     58
relative domain names, 56
reload plug-in, 95, 107
reload subdirective
   in file plug-in, 40, 57
   in hosts plug-in, 61
replace directive for go.mod for CoreDNS, 177
replicas for autoscaling clusters in Kubernetes,
   105
resolution, 12
resolvers, 5
   functions of, 11
resource records, 9
   contents of record types, 17-26
     A record, 17
     AAAA record, 18
     CNAME record, 18
     MX record, 19
     NS record, 20
     PTR record, 23
     SOA record, 24-26
     SRV record, 21-23
   for headless services, 83
resources

About the Authors

John Belamaric is an experienced software engineer and architect with over 20 years of software design and development experience. He works on the Google Cloud team, focused on Kubernetes and GKE. He is also a core maintainer of CoreDNS, a CNCF project that provides dynamic, DNS-based service discovery in Kubernetes and other container and cloud stacks.

He is a senior staff software engineer at Google, holds three patents, and is a co-author of *OpenStack Cloud Application Development* (O'Reilly).

Cricket Liu graduated from the University of California, Berkeley, that great bastion of free speech, unencumbered Unix, and cheap pizza. He joined Hewlett-Packard after graduation and worked for HP for nine years.

Cricket began managing the hp.com zone after the Loma Prieta earthquake forcibly transferred the zone's management from HP Labs to HP's Corporate Offices (by cracking a sprinkler main and flooding a Labs computer room). Cricket was host-master@hp.com for over three years, and then joined HP's Professional Services Organization to cofound HP's Internet Consulting Program.

Cricket left HP in 1997 to form Acme Byte & Wire, a DNS consulting and training company, with his friend Matt Larson. Network Solutions acquired Acme in June 2000, and later the same day merged with VeriSign. Cricket worked for a year as director of DNS product management for VeriSign Global Registry Services.

Cricket joined Infoblox, a company that develops DNS, DHCP, and IP Address Management solutions, in March, 2003. He is currently their chief DNS architect and a senior fellow. He's been reassured that they mean "senior" in the respectful sense, not in the "senior discount" sense.

Colophon

The animal on the cover of *Learning CoreDNS* is the comber fish *(Serranus cabrilla)*, a saltwater fish found in the Mediterranean and Black seas, as well as along the eastern Atlantic coast from the British Isles to the tip of South Africa.

The comber fish typically is a sandy brown color with white vertical stripes along its oval-shaped body. This fish can often be found hunting on the bottom of the coastal shelf, among the rocks, grass, or coral. Mainly a solitary fish, the comber is rarely found in small groups. It feeds on various fishes and crustaceans, and is surprisingly fast when pursuing its prey.

Each comber fish is a hermaphrodite; when a pair spawns, one fish acts as a male and the other acts as a female. The spawning season is controlled by the moon's phase, and occurs from February to July with a peak in May.

While the comber fish's current conservation status is designated as of Least Concern, many of the animals on O'Reilly covers are endangered; all of them are important to the world.

The cover illustration is by Karen Montgomery, based on a black and white engraving from *Meyers Kleines Lexicon*. The cover fonts are Gilroy Semibold and Guardian Sans. The text font is Adobe Minion Pro; the heading font is Adobe Myriad Condensed; and the code font is Dalton Maag's Ubuntu Mono.

O'REILLY®

There's much more
where this came from.

Experience books, videos, live online
training courses, and more from O'Reilly
and our 200+ partners—all in one place.

Learn more at oreilly.com/online-learning

Milton Keynes UK
Ingram Content Group UK Ltd.
UKHW050144230424
441576UK00008B/503